A Certain Clarity

A Certain Clarity

Selected Poems

Lawrence Joseph

FARRAR STRAUS GIROUX / NEW YORK

Farrar, Straus and Giroux

120 Broadway, New York 10271

Printed in the United States of America

First edition, 2020

Library of Congress Cataloging-in-Publication Data
Names: Joseph, Lawrence, 1948– author.
Title: A certain clarity : selected poems / Lawrence Joseph.
Description: First Edition. | New York : Farrar, Straus and Giroux, 2020. | Includes index. | Summary:
    "A selection of poems from the celebrated poet and lawyer"—Provided by publisher.
Identifiers: LCCN 2019046727 | ISBN 9780374261122 (hardcover)
Subjects: LCGFT: Poetry.
Classification: LCC PS3560.O775 C47 2020 | DDC 811/.54—dc2
LC record available at https://lccn.loc.gov/2019046727

Designed by Crisis

Our books may be purchased in bulk for promotional, educational, or
business use. Please contact your local bookseller or the Macmillan
Corporate and Premium Sales Department at 1-800-221-7945, extension
5442, or by e-mail at MacmillanSpecialMarkets@macmillan.com.

www.fsgbooks.com
www.twitter.com/fsgbooks
www.facebook.com/fsgbooks

10 9 8 7 6 5 4 3 2 1

*In memory of my mother, Clara Francis Joseph,
and my father, Joseph Alexander Joseph*

CONTENTS

from So Where Are We? (2017)

Shouting
at No One

(1983)

I was appointed the poet of heaven.

It was my duty to describe
Theresa's small roses
as they bent in the wind.

I tired of this
and asked you to let me
write about something else.
You ordered, "Sit
in the trees where the angels sleep
and copy their breaths
in verse."

So I did,
and soon I had a public following:

Saint Agnes with red cheeks,
Saint Dorothy with a moon between her fingers
and the Hosts of Heaven.

You said, "You've failed me."
I told you, "I'll write lovelier poems,"
but, you answered,
"You've already had your chance:

you will be pulled from a womb
into a city."

THEN

Joseph Joseph breathed slower
as if that would stop
the pain splitting his heart.
He turned the ignition key
to start the motor and leave
Joseph's Food Market to those
who wanted what was left.
Take the canned peaches,
take the greens, the turnips,
drink the damn whiskey
spilled on the floor,
he might have said.
Though fire was eating half
Detroit, Joseph could only think
of how his father,
with his bad legs, used to hunch
over the cutting board
alone in light particled
with sawdust behind
the meat counter, and he began
to cry. Had you been there
you would have been thinking
of the old Market's wooden walls
turned to ash or how Joseph's whole arm
had been shaking as he stooped
to pick up an onion,

and you would have been afraid.
You wouldn't have known
that soon Joseph Joseph would stumble,
his body paralyzed an instant
from neck to groin.
You would simply have shaken your head
at the tenement named "Barbara" in flames
or the Guardsman with an M-16
looking in the window of Dave's Playboy Barbershop,
then closed your eyes
and murmured, This can't be.
You wouldn't have known
it would take nine years
before you'd realize the voice howling in you
was born then.

IT WILL RAIN ALL DAY

Breakfast at Buck's Eat Place;
a portrait of Henry Ford,
two eggs, hash browns,
sour coffee. Afterwards
I walk out on Vernor Avenue,
"looks like a river in the rain,"
the signs from small stores hanging
over the wet sidewalks like trees.
But rivers are not passed over
by a woman wearing a windbreaker
with flags sewn on both shoulders,
muttering to herself, head down,
or an unshaven man older
than he is, his body slanting
as if he's about to fall
headlong into a dream.
Neither looks at me waiting
at the light, in my car,
as windshield wipers eliminate
the stars of water.
Along the cemetery, poplars
look upward with thousands
of eyes into the rain
that comes down on the hills of lime
and coal, reminding me of Metz,
but the wind

that lifted rhododendrons that April
isn't here with me. What
do I want, driving through streets
past bars where fifty-year-old
truck drivers sip whiskey
and don't feel like talking,
past houses where chimney smoke
reveals fires and rooms I will
never know? On Fort Street
I pass the bar with "Fight Poverty—
Drink & Dance" scrawled in white paint
across its windowless front,
and then a block-long building,
windows knocked in, wires ripped
from the walls, toilet bowls
covered with dirt and spiderwebs.
It will rain all day.
I see a large crane lifting
a railroad car, piles of bald tires,
the two towers of Saint Anne's
where, in a corner, there are crutches,
body braces, and letters written
to acknowledge miracles. I want
all this to come to an end
or a beginning, I want to look
into the black eyes of the lone woman
waiting for a bus and say
something, I want my memory
to hold this air, so I can make

the hills with white hair
and the clouds breaking into blackness
my own, carry them with me
like the letters and icons
immigrants take in suitcases
to strange countries.

NOT YET

When my father breathed
unevenly, I, a child,
breathed unevenly, I prayed
in Saint Maron
Maronite Catholic Church
for the world to change.
When I saw my father's tears
I did not pray;
I hated our market
where the bullet
missed his heart,
I hoped the mists exhaled
by the Vale of Esk
in a country of lakes
four thousand miles away
would be mine.
That was before
Lopez whispered through his rotten teeth
behind a maze of welding guns,
"You're colored, like me,"
before I knew
so much anger,
so much need
to avenge the holy cross
and the holy card
with its prayers for the dead,

so many words
I have no choice to say.
Years without enough to make me
stop talking—
I want it all.
I don't want
the angel inside me, sword in hand,
to be silent.
Not yet.

FOG

All day the air was fog;
couldn't see
the barbed wire, rusting
scraps, stacks
and stacks of pallets,
the tar paper roof
of Dreamer's shack,
the underground
caverns of salt hardening
around bones.

        The fog says,
Who will save
Detroit now?
A toothless face
in a window shakes No,
sore fingers
that want to be still
say, Not me.
Not far away from where
Youmna lies
freezing in bed,
rolling her eyes, declaring,
This is a place!
the remains of mountains
wait to be moved
through smokestacks
into air.

THERE IS A GOD WHO HATES US SO MUCH

I

I was pulled from the womb
into this city.

I learned words when my grandfather
lost both legs.

Before the altar of God
I spent hours on my knees.
I felt God's anger
when my semen spilled into my hand.
I ate God's body.
I promised to never sin.

I learned sadness from my mother's eyes.
I learned silence in the dust
a woman hid behind
to cover her face of scars
I learned blood from my father
fallen to a wooden floor,
a thief's bullet inside him.
He lived to warn me to forget.

After that I sucked darkness.

II

Years were a breath.

Alone, with whirring metal,
clattering and pounding
I could not abstract,
smells that tortured me,
I felt my words close inside me
like marrow.

I was a system of laws
I hated, a boy
afraid of burning
in a city that was burning
as my father cried
and my mother whispered in my hair.

14

III

I am the poet of my city.

I am the earth that burns the air,
those who talk to themselves,
blood and grease on hands.
I need to know
why I do not want to remember.

In dreams I run through streets
terrified, away
from mouths that hate me,
my face washed with fear.
In dreams I kill
so I will not be killed.

The city is the shadow
strapped to my back.

I am the poet of that shadow.

IV

Mother says, "Don't
think about it too much."

Father splashes cold water on his face,
vomits his nightmare:
he sweat before a man
who wanted to kill him.

I hold a holy candle and a palm branch,
kiss the feet of a statue,
drink holy water,
imagine my body without words,
pray to be able to sacrifice
like the saint
with arrows in his heart.

God gives the world
the brown and black frost
the city climbs through
to stars no one can see.

V

That is where I am now, in this city
where there are hours of sun
above the horizon and dirt in the air
that makes me want to holler.

There is a God who hates us so much:
we are given ears to hear ribs kicked in,
we are given eyes to see eyes close
before a city that burns itself to death.

Father shouts until his throat cracks,
the river stops in its sludge,
I pray to know what to pray for:
there is a God who hates us so much.

I was born in this city and live in this city
and know this city like no one else.
Who makes me eat my words and makes my eyes pain:
I measure you according to your creation.

IN THE TENTH YEAR OF WAR

I bend
over the machine. Heat
and oil
tune my inner ear. I'm
not ashamed, I
hang my head in
anticipation. Father,
steel smooth and silver,
make my brain new,
Jesus, the dirt on the walls
is coming from my body,
and love,
the spirit coming from your body—
everywhere you look now,
everything you touch,
it's good.
When,
in the tenth year of war
I prayed for help
and no one came,
I danced before the machine.

WHEN YOU'VE BEEN HERE LONG ENOUGH

You breathe yellow smoke, you breathe lead
beside the river, talking out loud to no one.

A rat slips by you into the cold green water.
No longer, at six o'clock Mass, do you kneel,

body bent over and swaying, chanting,
"Mea culpa, mea culpa, mea maxima culpa,"

offering your sorrow to the Poor Souls in Purgatory,
no longer do you dream of your mother as a child

waiting for a streetcar in the snow, praying
to Saint Jude to cure her sister's paralyzed hand.

When the waitress argues, "What you do is
hang them, downtown, in Grand Circus Park—

that would keep them off the streets," you don't answer.
You hear about the woman who twenty-five years ago touched

the back of your head and said, "It's shaped
just like your daddy's." She just sat there

and watched blood spray from her cut wrist all over
her room in the La Moon Manor Hotel. You just

shake your head. You're not surprised.
Because, when you've been here long enough

no one can make you believe the Black Cat
Dream Book provides your winning number.

Heaven answers your prayers with dust and you swallow it.
Alone, early morning, on the Wyoming Crosstown bus,

you feel the need to destroy, like everyone else,
as the doors open and no one comes on.

DO WHAT YOU CAN

In the Church of I AM she hears there is a time to heal,
but her son, Top Dog of the Errol Flynn gang,

doesn't lay down his sawed-off shotgun,
the corn she planted in the field where

the Marvel Motor Car factory once was
doesn't grow with pigweed and cocklebur.

When someone in the Resurrection Lounge laughs,
"Bohunk put the two-foot dogfish in the whore's hand,"

someone's daughter whispers, "Fuck you,"
places a half-smoked cigarette in her coat pocket,

swings open the thick wooden door, and walks
into air that freezes when it hears frost

coming from Sault Sainte Marie. Driving, I see
a shed of homing pigeons, get out of my car to look.

I answer, "What you care?" to a woman who shouts, "What you want?"
Beside the Church of Saint John Nepomocene

an old man, hunched and cold, prays, "Mother of God"
to a statue of the Virgin Mary

surrounded by a heart-shaped rosary
of fifty-three black and six white bowling balls.

Where the Ford and Chrysler freeways cross
a sign snaps, 5,142,250,

the number of cars produced so far this year in America.
Not far away, on Beaufait Street,

a crowd gathers to look at the steam
from blood spread on the ice. The light red,

I press the accelerator to keep the motor warm.
I wonder if they know

that after the jury is instructed
on the Burden of Persuasion and the Burden of Truth,

that after the sentence of twenty to thirty years comes down,
when the accused begs, "Lord, I can't do that kind of time,"

the judge, looking down, will smile and say,
"Then do what you can."

IT'S NOT ME SHOUTING AT NO ONE

Before dawn, on the street again,
beneath sky that washes me
with ice, smoke, metal.
I don't want to think
the bullet pierced my shoulder,
the junkie's rotten teeth
laughed, his yellow hair froze.
I'm careful: I smoke
Turkish tobacco cigarette butts,
I drink a lot to piss a lot,
I fry the pig in its own fat,
eat the knuckles, brain, and stomach;
I don't eat the eyes!
Always four smokestacks
burning bones, somewhere
tears that won't stop,
everywhere blood becomes
flesh that wants to say something.
It's not me shouting at no one
in Cadillac Square: it's God
roaring inside me, afraid
to be alone.

Curriculum Vitae

(1988)

IN THE AGE OF POSTCAPITALISM

The disabled garment worker
who explains to his daughter
he's God the Holy Spirit
and lonely and doesn't care
if he lives or dies;
the secret sarcoma shaped like a flower
in the bowels of a pregnant woman;
ashes in the river, a floating chair,
long, white, shrieking cats,
the watch that tells Zurich,
Jerusalem, and Peking time;
and the commodities broker
nervously smiling, mouth slightly twitching
when he says to the police he's forgotten
where he left his Mercedes:
everything attaches itself to me today.
Thirty million—the American
Broadcasting Corporation World News
conservatively estimates—
murders already this century.
Whether the public debt
may have affected case history
Number 51's excuse that she was abandoned
on the pier by a dolphin
and the question "What Has Become of
the Question of 'I'"

are topics for discussion
at the Institute for Political Economy.
I know all about the transmigration of souls.
I know about love and about strife.
To delight in a measured phrase,
to bank the rage in the gut,
to speak more softly,
to waken at three in the morning to think only of her
—in the age of postcapitalism.
Yellow and gray dusk thickens around the Bridge.
Rain begins to slant between
the chimneys and the power plant.
I don't feel like changing,
or waiting anymore either,
and I don't believe we're dreaming
this October sixth, in New York City,
during the nineteen eighties.

CURRICULUM VITAE

I might have been born in Beirut,
not Detroit, with my right name.
Grandpa taught me to love to eat.
I am not Orthodox, or Sunni,
Shiite, or Druse. Baptized
in the one true Church, I too
was weaned on Saint Augustine.
Eisenhower never dreamed I wore
corrective shoes. Ford Motor Co.
never cared I'd never forgive
Highland Park, River Rouge, Hamtramck.
I memorized the Baltimore Catechism.
I collected holy cards, prayed
to a litany of saints to intercede
on behalf of my father who slept
through the sermon at seven o'clock Mass.
He worked two jobs, believed
himself a failure. My brother
believed himself, my sister denied.
In the fifth grade Sister Victorine,
astonished, listened to me recite
from the Book of Jeremiah.
My voice changed. I wanted women.
The Jesuit whose yellow fingers
cracked with the stink of Camels
promised me eternal punishment.

How strange I was, with impure thoughts,
brown skin, obsessions.
You could tell by the way I walked
I possessed a lot of soul,
you could tell by the way I talked
I didn't know when to stop.
After I witnessed stabbings
outside the gym, after the game,
I witnessed fire in the streets.
My head set on fire in Cambridge,
England, in the Whim Café.
After I applied Substance and Procedure
and Statements of Facts
my head was heavy, was earth.
Now years have passed since I came
to the city of great fame.
The same sun glows gray on two new rivers.
Tears I want do not come.
I remain many different people
whose families populate half Detroit;
I hate the racket of the machines,
the oven's heat, curse
bossmen behind their backs.
I hear the inmates' collective murmur
in the jail on Beaubien Street.
I hear myself say, "What explains
the Bank of Lebanon's liquidity?"
think, "I too will declare
a doctrine upon whom the loss

of language must fall regardless
whether Wallace Stevens
understood senior indebtedness
in Greenwich Village in 1906."
One woman hears me in my sleep
plead the confusions of my dream.
I frequent the Café Dante, earn
my memories, repay my moods.
I am as good as my heart.
I am as good as the unemployed
who wait in long lines for money.

BY THE WAY

What I saw was impossible
together. Only months between
the factories, furnaces
with hissing bronze pipes, smoke
streamed across flat skies,
and a woman named Mimi di Nescemi, who exits
in black silk trousers, delicate heels;
a man who says his name is Ra
wrapped in blankets in a cardboard box
on Gold Street. I tried to explain.

On Saturday night, January 10, 1970,
at eight minutes past eight,
in Joseph's Market my father perceived
how desperate the man was
—he'd kill. The bullet missed
the heart and the spinal cord,
miraculously, the doctor said.
Everything eventually would be all right.
The event went uncelebrated among hundreds
of felonies in that city that day.

At lunch at the Broad Street Club
I couldn't stop looking at
the woman at the table across from me.
Beige-colored suit, blouse

unbuttoned two buttons, I could tell
she was sensual and smart and that
her presence hadn't gone unnoticed
by two bankers whose conversation
on floating exchange rates and computers
I couldn't help but overhear.

I couldn't help but overhear
my thoughts and opinions.
My starting point? Not Plato.
What if poverty and anger
and the desire for thrills,
and tribal attitudes, exist
not only on the streets but innately
—inherent, if you will,
within the boundaries of the nation,
social and economic classes, our time?

On public television, on a program
on national affairs, Mr. Getty
distinctly recalls his director's
emphasis: at one hundred dollars a share
or higher, the museum was a seller
not a buyer. "Which is a rhyme,"
Mr. Getty explains. "Put me among
the circle of poets for that.
That's the lowest circle
in Dante's hell, by the way."

In the Third Circle of Alexandria's
Department of Irrigation Services,
Special Clerk Constantine Kavafis
aggravated his imagination, thought
too much about the poet Lamon's
popularity (the rave of all
literary Beirut), and interpreted
the Asian blood in his veins.
In another circle, poets punctuate
their remarks with tics and odd sneezes.

In some circles, poets whip themselves
under every conceivable influence into mania
to advertise. In another room
a beautiful woman toward whom men always
try to be personal; which secrets,
which consciousness, cause her aloofness?
In the lowest circle in hell the Republic
has been betrayed, by the way.
In the lowest circle, shadows
seize skulls with their teeth.

SAND NIGGER

In the house in Detroit
in a room of shadows
when Grandma reads her Arabic newspaper
it is difficult for me to follow her
word by word from right to left
and I do not understand
why she smiles about the Jews
who won't do business in Beirut
"because the Lebanese
are more Jew than Jew,"
or whether to believe her
that if I pray
to the holy card of Our Lady of Lebanon
I will share the miracle.
Lebanon is everywhere
in the house: in the kitchen
of steaming pots, leg of lamb
in the oven, plates of kousa,
hushwee rolled in cabbage,
dishes of olives, tomatoes, onions,
roasted chicken, and sweets;
at the card table in the sunroom
where Grandpa teaches me
to wish the dice across the backgammon board
to the number I want;
Lebanon of mountains and sea,

of pine and almond trees,
of cedars in the service
of Solomon, Lebanon
of Babylonians, Phoenicians, Arabs, Turks,
and Byzantines, of the one-eyed
monk, Saint Maron,
in whose rite I am baptized;
Lebanon of my mother
warning my father not to let
the children hear,
of my brother who hears
and from whose silence
I know there is something
I will never know; Lebanon
of Grandpa giving me my first coin
secretly, secretly
holding my face in his hands,
kissing me and promising me
the whole world.
My father's vocal cords bleed;
he shouts too much
at his brother, his partner,
in the grocery store that fails.
I hide money in my drawer, I have
the talent to make myself heard.
I am admonished to learn,
never to dirty my hands
with sawdust and meat.
At dinner, a cousin

describes his niece's head
severed with bullets, in Beirut,
in civil war. "More than
an eye for an eye," he demands,
breaks down, and cries.
My uncle tells me to recognize
my duty, to use my mind,
to bargain, to succeed.
He turns the diamond ring
on his finger, asks if
I know what asbestosis is,
"the lungs become like this,"
he says, holding up a fist;
he is proud to practice
law which "distributes
money to compensate flesh."
Outside the house my practice
is not to respond to remarks
about my nose or the color of my skin.
"Sand nigger," I'm called,
and the name fits: I am
the light-skinned nigger
with black eyes and the look
difficult to figure—a look
of indifference, a look to kill—
a Levantine nigger
in the city on the strait
between the great lakes Erie and St. Clair
which has a reputation

for violence, an enthusiastically
bad-tempered sand nigger
who waves his hands, nice enough
to pass, Lebanese enough
to be against his brother,
with his brother against his cousin,
with cousin and brother
against the stranger.

RUBAIYAT

All the stories about killing, burned bones, the smoke
from burning bones, a body tied by a rope fastened to a Mercedes
flying above the ground, cut-up body in a nylon bag,
black hoods, hallucinations, stylized hair and pure gold chains,

a report, according to the government official, forty-two
forced into the church and hacked to death with axes on the altar,
accounts confirmed by government officials, a five-year-old boy
discovered nailed to a doorway in the form of a cross.

And what do you think you're doing when you want the names
and the years of the history, who begot whom and who made
which flesh which words that hate for which particular reasons
that compel the pride of the horrors of the oppressed?

That's how the brain talks, evil in its wakefulness.
It's just too crazy and it's too much and not unreal.
Fourteen years it's been now since Beirut's dust and the Shouf's sun
repressed. The crippled child without eyelashes spoke.

His face blue, his words didn't leave his mouth—
this is twelve years before Corporal McMahon in the bunker
"The Psycho Ward" beside the airport below Souk-al-Gharb
pokes at his C-rations, answers back home he liked to hunt geese.

Uncle Shikory three times a week took a bus to Beirut.
He did some deals in the back of some store. Talked slowly
in French about how little he remembered his brother, my grandfather,
Angele, his daughter, frail and small, her husband dead ten years

—a cerebral hemorrhage. She wears layers of black.
He was only thirty-five and she isn't young. I hear her
weeping in the dark. Her eyes deep dark, sad and heavy.
She likes me—my moods. Once she touched my shoulders,

whispered, *d'accord, d'accord.* I've never forgotten that.
When I try consciously not to forget I surely will exhaust
the imagination. April. A year ago. In the Consul's residence.
Yasine Aballah Bacha. He asks if I know his family.

He too studied law—he and one of his bodyguards, Yousef Farsane.
Chartoun? He showed me an official map. Here it is
where the road from Damascus turns before Aleih. Captured
for obvious strategic reasons. At least twelve massacred,

one hundred forty-seven houses and the church destroyed.
I insult him if I don't smoke the Marlboro he offers,
don't drink Scotch whiskey first, before I drink coffee.
He calls the servant, a tall girl from Mauritania.

She became his when he was the Ambassador there, he says.
Lebanon is like Kafka, he says—emphasizing Kafka.
I should get in touch with him when I come to Los Angeles again;
he would like to introduce me to some of his friends.

You say the Shah of Baabda sits like a crow on the head
of the gangster from Syria who kisses both ears of the Sheikh
of Zaghorta, who secretly covets the Prince of Moukharta's access
through State Department intermediaries to the King of Israel—

who cares that your politics change, that you change,
that a sharp nausea plugs your chest, blood quickened
with the harmonies of numbers counted, realized, and forgotten?
It is no time to be uncertain about what has happened or what can.

What has Angele seen? What has she had to put into her brain?
Uncle Shikory's insane; the nuns in the mountain take care of him
Where is Angele? Gone with the others into the mountain?
Where is Angele? Her eyes were heavy. She wore black ten years.

THAT'S ALL

I work and I remember. I conceive
a river of cracked hands above Manhattan.

No spirit leaped with me in the womb.
No prophet explains why Korean women

thread Atomic Machinery's machines
behind massive, empty criminal tombs.

Why do I make my fire my heart's blood,
two or three ideas thought through

to their conclusions, make my air
dirty the rain around towers of iron,

a brown moon, the whole world?
My power becomes my sorrow.

Truth? My lies are sometimes true.
Firsthand, I now see the God

whose witness is revealed in tongues
before the Exchange on Broad Street

and the transfer of 2,675,000,000 dollars
by tender offer are acts of the mind,

and the calculated truths of First
National City Bank. Too often

I think about third cousins in the Shouf.
I also often think about the fact that

in 1926, after Céline visited
the Ford Rouge foundry and wrote

his treatise on the use of physically
inferior production line workers,

an officially categorized "displaced person"
tied a handkerchief around his face

to breathe the smells and the heat
in a manner so as not to destroy

his lungs and brain for four years
until he was laid off. I don't

meditate on hope and despair.
I don't deny the court that rules

my race is Jewish or Abyssinian.
In good times I transform myself

into the sun's great weight, in bad times
I make myself like smoke on flat wastes.

I don't know why I choose who I am:
I work and I remember, that's all.

AN AWFUL LOT WAS HAPPENING

When you come down to particulars everything's more complicated.
Fervent gestures in the South U restaurant, even the Greeks
behind the counter listen. Burned draft cards,
lamb's blood poured over files at the downtown draft board
—acts of resistance, moral values begun.

Saint Augustine in *De Trinitate* didn't see memory structured
by public events. A great moment in my life—not purple clouds
which excited my longings in Nichols Arboretum;
instead, the rumor cancer spread through Lyndon Johnson's brain.
Saint Augustine in his *Enchiridion ad Laurentium* didn't see

her dress and bra across the only chair in my small room
at One Thousand Four Olivia. I couldn't comprehend
whether more words might mean more, my greed, untrained,
not yet certain of its justifications.
And there was war. And from the bluffs above the Huron River

rain of starlight above Ann Arbor's lights, three, four
bell chimes ringing in the Tower. It wasn't Rome.
She dizzied me with excessive desires and thoughts.
What I wanted from all my talk of beauty, she said, was power,
and because of it, she said, I'd cause much suffering.

Although I never bragged misery—maybe once. I was serious.
What was I supposed to do when I heard you could be beaten or worse
in the neighborhood in Detroit between Linwood and Dexter,
the color of your eyes wrong. These are facts.
Professor Fuller's response that no one taught them to be quiet.

Glass from the bank's large plated windows all over the street.
I telephoned—line busy; tried again a few minutes later
—no answer. Where is she?—the verge of tears.
Swinburnian dactyls merely went through my ears. Advocated
concision, spatial range, temporal disposition of simple language.

And didn't the spokesman for the Black Action Movement
also receive a number over three hundred in the draft lottery
and attend graduate school? —I came back.
Three years later, every space turned inside out.
January, noon, beams of light across you shake out. Confused,

whirling joy when you slid off me. I leaned
again to embrace you. Uniform Commercial Code on the table.
On the dresser, a cup of coffee, tulips in a vase.
How to explain to myself how much I love you.
In the Law Quadrangle—my peer. He commanded Marines

in the Anhoa Basin. What did I know—what hookworms are like.
What it's like to shoot a Viet Cong, popped from a hole, in the eye.
A piece of metal in your kidney. It's too easy
to be sheep, he concludes, softly. Or too difficult,
I add, softly. He stares at me and whispers something.

When I answered I intended to maintain freedom my brother was riled.
What, or who, collides in you beside whose body I sleep?
No work at Tool & Die, Motors, Transmission, or Tractor
while the price of American crude rises another dollar.
There really wasn't enough work anywhere. And there was war

God the spirit of holy tongues couldn't release me from,
or from my dumbness. Pressured—delirious—
from too much inductive thinking, I waited for
the image in whose presence the heart opens and opens
and lived to sleep well; of necessity assessed earth's profit

in green and red May twilight. —You came toward me
in your black skirt, white blouse rolled at the sleeves.
Anticipation of your eyes, your loose hair!
My elementary needs—to cohere, to control.
An awful lot was happening and I wanted more.

LONDON

Aged malt whiskey and cigarettes
    consumed to enhance consciousness
—read Blake. You can't regulate
    the price of necessaries
without destruction. In a bar
    a few streets from the British Museum
across the table from Oxford's
    latest rising literary star;
not much older than you, his
    history is already impressive.
"There are rules, aren't there,"
    he shrugs, agitatedly,
"and decorum, and irony,"
    he clears his throat and, then,
vanishes behind the Royal Exchange,
    beyond the intent stare
of someone, somewhere, aggrieved
    and the student from the Polytechnic
who laughs after he announces
    he's schizophrenic before he, too,
vanishes down a small lane
    behind the old synagogue
away from where you walk alone
    along Victoria Embankment.
—The sky was low, always low,
    often clear, or raw. You were
the "you" aware of the spite

and the sorrow. Spirit
to the bone set loose, sensed,
    certain violence. Spirit
in the blood set loose, moved
    by cold smoke from the rows
evaporating. Those whose faces
    thrust forward, gaunt, no chins,
no more eyes—that kind of look
    possessed. It happened;
it wasn't misunderstanding when that woman
    said she never could have
had or have what you have,
    looked away, too sensitive.
An argument on the last train
    from Cambridge to King's Cross
about—the extent of His
    Lordship's estate. The poplar's shadow
darker than the bluish light,
    spread across complete silence
on the Green at midnight.
    The fact, in Glasgow, straight
razors were means to threaten
    or deter; the fact we are victims
of our truths was true.
    You ought not to have been
what you were, what you
    might have been was a simple fate
in a bag of wind. Nothingness
    erupted. Everything foretold.

ANY AND ALL

You draw nearer to see her more closely,
the blind woman by the bronze doors

of the old Merchants Bank, her mouth
wide open as if in a silent roar,

several dollars stuffed in the pockets
of her mink coat. She is easy to forget

a few days later when you think of her
—not long. The phone is ringing.

You put Byrdman on hold. Polen
wants you in his office immediately.

The lawyers from Mars and the bankers
from Switzerland have arrived to close the deal,

the money in their heads articulated
to the debt of the state of Bolivia.

How much later the Croatian woman
who empties the wastebaskets laughs

when you answer you've been better
and you've been worse. How much sooner

you're told not to tell anyone Byrdman's
grandfather was a Jew. How much No. 54

Wall Street, emblematic reality of extreme
speculations and final effects.

The other evening a party in the West Sixties
you say as much. None of them knows

what any of it is worth, you say to yourself
later, spitting into an unexpected breeze.

Yellow moons of streetlamps on Ninth Avenue
obscured by atmospheric soot and fog,

in the Twenties empty windows of butcher shops,
factories and warehouses without names,

no taxis, the green light behind the window
of a corner bar. A young man sporting muscles,

a woman he might own on his arm, clearly
doesn't like the way you look or look at him,

lets his leash out enough for his wolf dog
to just nip your leg. Another day

you contemplate your strategy:
think about how they think about you

thinking about them and the look on your face
to prove you have the proper attitude.

Let no laughter reveal moods. Let
Charlotte Stone reveal that her father

over the weekend purchased a peninsula in Rhode Island
for Harry and her, let her teeth

be too large and too gray: there is blood
and there is bloodletting; this is not your blood.

Shut the door and wait. Someone else's father
forgives you when you know not what you do,

reminds you, "He's a weasel but he's my friend."
You're a monkey and you work for him,

decide for him whether his clauses should be restrictive,
whether to replace every "any" with "all."

MY GRANDMA WEIGHED ALMOST NOTHING

It was that April morning that the weight
of tumor mass eroded her frontal bone
through her dura to the brain's substance,

through the corridor of junipers on the road
to Aleih, before the blood of the Great War
dried, and the priest beat Tanous's head

in Hadeth? or was it Chartoun? her cousin
with his large brown, black eyes agreed
and she agreed, in that month of mists,

although Najla burned with whooping cough
and the sun, and mosquitoes ruined the olives,
in that hour of dark blue night, the year

1912 or 1913, wrapped in blankets while sea
turned over toward Marseilles and the island
Ellis became the beautiful valley and the lakes

Ontario and Erie, and the voice on the train
said, Detroit, and she said that word again,
Detroit, before the cold air behind the maples

on Livernois cracked yellow, before Alfred,
in his new suit, bragged Purple Gang
to Angele, in the store on Cass and Temple.

—She couldn't hold herself up, or sleep
and dream dreams she didn't want. She rubbed
her bald skull. My grandma weighed almost

nothing—arms folded around her like sea
and its algae, old sea softened into a Boulevard
or heat or sleep and silence ten times

pain that made her weight her bones
and one or two tears she cried alone
in Women's Hospital that April—then died.

ON NATURE

To proceed: whether results are evident
because they're results. Mists
from chromeplate parts precipitate
ulcers of the skin and cancer.
Raw, hard sun becoming stronger.
Should I save my pity for myself?
Do to others what's been done to you?
Unlimited desires at age thirty-seven
moved to tears before a rose.
It makes sense the state-controlled regime
enters into a series of contracts
with private corporations to produce
and market its oil resources.
The data actually prove it's difficult
to draw conclusions on the fate
of the lower middle class. Will
the sophora tree maintain its distinctness?
Free potatoes, trucked from another state,
feeding those reconciled to their doom.
Pork fat? Ten to twenty-four million tons of dust,
loss of light north of the equator,
temperature drop of eighteen to fifty-five degrees
depending on the season. August afternoon
velveted with drink, softened
yellow; floundering marsh, iron river,
blue, heavy air in the bloodstream.

Everyone has some, no one has enough,
but if you have the will you'll be taken care of.
When imported shoes mean the state
of the economy isn't prosperous?
Water with nothing but a little lemon in it.
The woman in bed turning toward
her husband drowsing in a chair?
You get nothing for nothing and a rat's
human as a cat, and the bird
with wild open wings creates a counterlight.
Cool metallic shimmering on the avenue.
Your eyes I can't take mine from.
Will you love me more if I remain silent?
Even the belief in metamorphosis
after a while doesn't bother me.

THERE I AM AGAIN

I see it again, at dusk, half darkness in its brown light,
large tenements with pillars on Hendrie beside it,

the gas station and garage on John R beside it,
sounds of a cappella from a window somewhere, pure, nearby it

pouring through the smell of fried pork to welcome
whoever enters it to do business.

Today, again, in the second year of the fifth recession
my father holds pickled feets, stomachs, and hearts,

I lift crates of okra and cabbages,
let down crates of buttermilk and beer,

bring live carp to the scale, and come, at last, to respect
the intelligence of roaches in barrels of bottles,

I sell the blood on the wooden floor after the robbery,
salt pork and mustard greens and Silver Satin wine,

but only if you pay, down, on the counter
money you swear you'll never hand over, only if,

for collateral, you don't forget you too may have to kill.
Today, again, in the third year of unlimited prosperity,

the Sunday night the city burns
I hear sirens, I hear broken glass, I believe

the shadow of my father's hand that touches my hair,
my cousin loading a carbine, my uncle losing his mind

today in a place the length of a pig's snout
in a time the depth of a cow's brain

in Joseph's Market on the corner of John R and Hendrie
there I am again: always, everywhere,

apron on, alone behind the cash register, the grocer's son
angry, ashamed, and proud as the poor with whom he deals.

FROM

Before
Our Eyes

(1993)

BEFORE OUR EYES

The sky almost transparent, saturated
manganese blue. Windy and cold.
A yellow line beside a black line,
the chimney on the roof a yellow line
behind the mountain ash on Horatio.
A circular cut of pink flesh hanging
in the shop. Fish, flattened, copper,
heads chopped off. The point is to bring
depths to the surface, to elevate
sensuous experience into speech
and the social contract. Ribbons of smoke
silhouette the pier, a navy of yachts
pounded by the river's green waves.
By written I mean made, by made I mean felt;
concealed things, sweet sleep of colors.
So you will be, perhaps appropriately,
dismissed for it, a morality of seeing,
laying it on. Who among the idealists
won't sit in the private domain,
exchange culture with the moneymakers?
Here's one with acute hypertension
ready to crack the pressure cuff,
there's the type whose hallucinatory
devolution of the history of tribes
is personalized. My grandpa? He never
contended where Lebanon's history

began, if the child prince was smuggled
by his mother to a Catholic family
in the Mountain where he passed his boyhood
in his father's religion, a Druse,
the most secret sect of Islam.
I received the news in Jerusalem—
the Beirut Easter radio event, the dancer
undulating to sounds of explosions
outside the studio. The future isn't Africa,
my friend, and Europe's a peninsula of Asia,
and your America's a creation of Europe,
he laughed, the newspaperman, pointing
his finger. Still, don't street smarts
matter? Waiting rooms, shopping centers,
after all, empty moods and emotions.
And no denial's built up inside me.
It was, I admit, more charged than
I thought at the time. More predetermined.
Silver and red scraps inside the air,
cascades of sublimated pig iron.
Language more discursive, a more sequential
expression, and I attested to it.
The old dying? The new not yet born? The old,
the new, you fool, aphorized by Henry Ford
in '22. First make the cars, the roads
will follow. Modes of production created
of their own accord. The process runs
of its own accord. Current and diaphanous
sight and sound, comprehended, but poetry

I know something about. The act of forming
imagined language resisting humiliation.
Fading browns and reds, a maroon glow,
sadness and brightness, glorified.
Voices over charred embankments, smell
of fire and fat. The pure metamorphic
rush through with senses, just as you said
it would be. The soft, subtle twilight
only the bearer feels, broken into angles,
best kept to oneself. For the time being
let's just keep to what's before our eyes.

ADMISSIONS AGAINST INTEREST

I

Taking my time, literal as I seemed, crazy
enough for silly disputes, actually Asiatically

sorry-eyed, reconciled finally
to the fact the January snow

behind the silver shed was only that,
the sudden sense you've seen it all before

appearing to take shape. For the likes of me
the weather wasn't any theory,

only conflagrations of the specks of a scene,
of rain the smell of smoldering soot,

clouds sweeping crimson down the street,
a physical thing. Bound by the Continual

Ministries of Thine Anger—a funny sight,
on both knees, all or nothing

outside in, wanting evil to disappear,
a complex character rattling off his complexity

the way, in Arabic, my grandmother would.
Mind you, though, my primary rule:

never use the word "I" unless you have to,
but sell it cheaply to survive.

   II

Now, what type of animal asks after facts?
—so I'm a lawyer. Maybe charming,

direct yet as circumspect as any other lawyer
going on about concrete forces of civil

society substantially beyond anyone's grasp
and about money. Things like "you too

may be silenced the way powerful
corporations silence, contractually"

attract my attention. The issue's
bifurcated. "Why divide the dead?"

the Foreign Minister asks, "what's one life
when you've lost twenty million?"

And if what has happened during my life
had been otherwise could I say

I would have seen it much differently?
Authority? Out of deeper strata

illuminations. A lot of substance
chooses you. And it's no one's business

judging the secrets each of us needs:
I don't know what I'd do without my Double.

III

So the times demanded figuring out,
and on winter evenings beams of violet

appeared, thin and violent. Gorgeous violet
avenue, gentle, frightened look. The state's agency

assigned to the task of measuring toxicological
effects on the sticky matter

of recollection cells doesn't have any idea.
The air roundabout the Bridge can't be

gold. "You know it makes you want to
shout," the girl on the bus, laughing, shouts,

throws both her hands up, the same song
tuned up on her radio, and I'm off into a mood again,

another internal swoon. So certain combinations
never before are worked on and hard,

knowing early on I could never act
as if I didn't think. My best cogitations

dwell in air so thick it weighs
on the skin, a solid complex, constrained

by this woman's clear fierce eyes wet
in this rain either with rain or with tears.

IV

And so I've had, vast and gray, the sky
my heart, amazed, determined by

the sight of a shimmering simulacrum,
undisturbed color. My admissions

against interest look smaller,
confirmations of another order.

My ancestors are on another plane,
never wholly innocent feeling any horror,

soul-contracted children of common cells,
never wholly distributed sensations

dejected into vertical visions and desire.
So I too am late at my singing,

too much to the point, but now I'm seeing
words are talk and words themselves

forms of feeling, rose-colored splashings
the ice-cold dawn, reliance upon

bare winds pouncing that dot of fire
inside compressed half-luminous air

deflected out of those places I see
formed into feeling, patches of light.

UNDER A SPELL

Now the governor of the Federal Reserve Bank
doesn't know how much more he can take
while my thoughts wander outside me and can't be grasped—
I'm under a spell. While the prisoners
on Death Row whose brain cells will reach
the point of boiling water during electrocution
receive blessings through cable television
and presidents and commissars devise
international housecleanings
history won't recognize for years,
the precedence of language and image preoccupies me too
under the influence of a spell.
Under a spell you have to remember
Monday morning of the insurrection,
the body in the ruins of Stanley's
Patent Medicine Store on John R
a block away from Joseph's Market,
when we argued time and space and memory are the same,
worked at The Rouge or The Axle,
read essays by an activist monk on nonviolence
unaware of the strains we placed on our souls,
skies always choked by gray clouds
moving at different speeds, slag piled
pink and black at the end of the streets.
Under a spell paradise opens again,
a labyrinth. The vistas down the cross streets

are slabs of sun. The confused time
we cried in each other's arms.
Returning at the end of the suffering
to myself who loves no one. Returning
years later to that smoky twilight, still easy to find,
the breezes and sea smells from the Hudson
unexpectedly surrounding us, your eyes
unusually blue. Only you—with whom I can't pretend—
see everything go through me. Nothing's said
when you turn and look through me.

OVER DARKENING GOLD

I

So here we are. Thieves stealing from thieves
in a society of complex spheres,
wondering what you should do. And still
stars blown outside the eye's corner.

II

The babies are asleep in beautiful lines.
But your eye's circuit is going so fast
we're no longer human. In that other place
a dog is still wailing in the background.

III

She said, "That's what I said." She said it.
"Desire isn't a form of sorrow," she said.
Around us wild metallic shimmering,
history, a subject, inside the sky.

IV

Inwards—and backwards, too. The difficult
memory of a divisive memory, killing
the order of the day. The state of the state
consumes the sublime ebony of the moon.

V

Ease up! No, ease down. You're right.
These days one must be especially careful.
The determined are constantly moving,
formed over gold, over darkening gold.

ABOUT THIS

I surfaced from my reflections to see
wartime. YOUR BANK ACCOUNT AND FUCKING COUNT

a sign on the mirror of Le Club Beirut,
an obvious object of interpretation during,

quote, the month that shook the world—
and here and in Paris the fashion news

this season color runs riot. Once again,
in the midst of delirium, my companions

on the subway, those who clean offices
all through the night, close their eyes,

Ash Wednesday-faced, much less anxious,
even more exhausted. That beauty's

green-gray eyes slanting like a cat's
must feel the battery of worldviews.

I do, and believe Nebuchadnezzar in his bunker
religiously is watching himself on Cable

Network News. Where's my sense of humor?
Prices are soaring in the futures pits.

There—over there are the Asian refugees
starting to tear apart the sewage pipes

under the villas to moisten their lips.
Here I squint into the twilight's blazes,

into stabs of dazzling dark radiations,
a set of sights attending my sunbath.

One of us, very old, stops uncontrollably
laughing, sighs, sighs, three, four times,

before starting in again. That rickety one
staring hard at the digital disc player

on display in the World Financial Center's
Palace of Palm Trees covets precision.

Gold (the old favorite in times of stress)
has relinquished its postinvasion gains.

Enough of a shooting war, military
expenditures, there may be no recession.

Is it true, the rumor that the new
instruments of equity are children, commodified?

That the Attorney General has bit off his tongue?
Those are—nails! that maniac wearing

wingtip shoes, turning a tattooed
cheek, throws at us while we talk about evil

outside, over burgundy, at the Cloisters.
This is August and September. This is wartime

bound to be, the social and money value
of human beings in this Republic clear

as can be in air gone pink and translucent
with high-flying clouds and white heat.

SENTIMENTAL EDUCATION

So no self-centered anarchism
was of use, too manic the sense
of economy, employment and inflation
curved. Detroit's achromatic
sky for a son of lower
middle class parents like me
glowed. My baptism by fire
in the ancient manner,
at my father's side in a burning city,
nothing sacramental about it.

Everything was—everything fast!
Strips of twilight shadow sheened
transparency and cast
a concisely stylized groove
you could count on
around the door to the dance.
War days conscientiously objected to,
the racial on me all the time,
I knew my place, you might say,
and white-hot ingots

in their molds, same time,
same place blue jays among the marigolds
held their own beside
the most terrible rage, tears wept

for no reason at all except
what might have been
—my mother's tears, for instance.
She doesn't sleep well
in this climate
composed of pale tints.

But first, back to Henry Ford.
Of the world-famous Highland Park Plant
Otto Moog, the German engineer,
in 1923 proclaimed (Vladimir
Lenin thought so too): "No symphony
compares to the music hammering
through the colossal workplace"
—proof, so to speak,
that speech propels the purposes
by which it's been shaped.

But back, first, to Marvin Gaye,
during an interview in Brussels.
"Remember the Turbans?" he asks,
laughing at the memory. "Cats
sported silk headdresses, sang up
a storm. Had this one hit tune,
'Please Let Me Show You Around Myself,'
the lyrics comparing enclosed
empty space to an open heart
showed me to appreciate language."

Back to, because you want to,
Grand Boulevard, excessive sky
hot and indigo, poured out
onto Hendrie. Inside the store,
Grandpa lifts you into his arms,
small as a single summer Sunday,
a kind of memory trance truly
dark, deep and dark, steel dark,
not as pure, but almost as pure,
as pure unattainable light.

What now? The palette's red.
The beggars wear red in their hair.
Red's contained in the place's currency.
The distance sustained between
subject and object looks red.
History, increasingly ephemeral,
is red. The switches of the music are
red while you mark the beat,
consistent with your education,
without any inner dispute.

OUT OF THE BLUE

Not that we lacked experience.
We simply had no talent for murder.
And then it was November again.

The air brisk and cold, lights clicked
softly in a burnished glow.
A world with its own wild system of desires.

Yet somehow more fragile.
In a completely different place
from its syntax, in fact—far ahead of it.

And who could not be struck by the notion?
A Great Wheel, gold and gray,
out of the blue, burst in flame.

Taking the shape of the moment.
Disappearing
in a crevice in the sky.

VARIATIONS ON VARIATIONS ON A THEME

I

Winter dragged on. Established remnants
fell apart, displaced by chaos, by functions.
Take the renowned banker who's murmuring
the socialization of money has become
an abstract force and he's nervous.
In the background, out of the ground of being,
a resident of the Hill, in her tin hut
at the end of the Manhattan Bridge, insists
she possesses a master's degree in English.

II

My friend the priest is studying Malcolm's
X, how Detroit Red decided to redesign
his sorrow—"the X a cross," he contends,
though none of it the gnosticism popularized
in certain circles. The way my friend
sees it, the species is undergoing
a cerebral mutation three distinct types
will survive: those who need to kill,
those who wait silently for transformation,
and those, the militants, seesawing
between the murderers and the victims.

III

Tell me about it! Molten copper
burned copper into an ethereal haze.
"My God," she added softly, "it seems
so terribly long ago." No, this afternoon,
I actually saw one of my peers
pour perfume over the body of a shadow.

IV

And that's the law. To bring to light
most hidden depths. The juror screaming
defendant's the devil staring at her
making her insane. The intense strain
phrasing the truth, the whole truth, nothing
but sentences, endless sentences.

V

No, I haven't forgotten—
to attend once more to words as words. I mean it.
Lips and skin remember,
a voice on the avenue
sensuous enough to touch.

VI

Gesticulating his head forward, poking
his baby finger, intonations arising
in a manner of speaking without agitation,
he says to her he doesn't understand
metempsychosis. In Walt Whitman's country,
pink and turquoise rhododendrons are
like porcelain after the rain, square,
dark-blinded windows behind her eyes,
hazel and hard, relenting at moments,
bound at the corners by minuscule lines.

VII

The war is a few days old. In the ever-blue
the sun continues its journey. You won't
kill their love of the actual. Let them go
conquer the world, march with Alexander:
there is Ur, the Chaldean city, a bronze
flake on a rock; there are millions, millions
plunged and numbed by dreams of blood.
It was then I had an attack of madness
—the eyewitness account the vanquished
appeared as if from a mirage of hot
oily smoke in search of someone
to surrender to—which almost made me smile.

VIII

What are you saying? This light is famous,
its sad, secret violet, and, this evening,
West and East rivers turned into one.
To remember and imagine at the same time
—that was the month of June that year.
Within the intensity you showed me
both cloudiness and transparency can be painted.

SOME SORT OF CHRONICLER I AM

Some sort of chronicler I am, mixing
emotional perceptions and digressions,

choler, melancholy, a sanguine view.
Through a transparent eye, the need, sometimes,

to see everything simultaneously
—strange need to confront everyone

with equal respect. Although the citizen
across the aisle on the Number Three

subway doesn't appreciate my respect.
Look at his eyes—both of them popping

from injections of essence of poppy;
listen to his voice bordering on a shrill.

His declaration: he's a victim of acquired
immuno-deficiency syndrome. His addiction

he acquired during the Indo-Chinese war.
Specified "underclass" by the Department of Labor

—he's underclass, all right: no class
if you're perpetually diseased and poor.

Named "blessed" by one of our Parnassians
known to make the egotistical sublime

—blessed, indeed; he's definitely blessed.
His wounds open, here, on the surface:

you might say he's shrieking his stigmata.
I know—you'd prefer I change the subject

(I know how to change the subject).
Battery Park's atmosphere changes

mists in which two children play and scratch
like a couple of kittens until the green

layers of light cover them completely,
a sense of anguished fulfillment arising

without me, beauty needled into awareness
without me, beauty always present in

what happened that instant her silhouette
moved across the wall, magnified sounds

her blouse made scraped against her skin
—workers, boarded storefronts, limousines

with tinted windows, windows with iron bars,
lace-patterned legs, someone without legs,

merged within the metathetical imagination
we're all part of, no matter how personal

we think we are. Has anyone considered
during the depression of 1921

Carlos Williams felt a physician's pain,
vowed to maintain the most compressed

expression of perceptions and ardors
—intrinsic, undulant, physical movement—

revealed in the speech he heard around him
(dynamization of emotions into imagined

form as a reality in itself),
Wallace Stevens—remember his work

covered high-risk losses—knowingly chose
during the bank closings of early '33

to suspend his grief between social planes
he'd transpose into thoughts, figures, colors

—you don't think he saw the woman beneath
golden clouds tortured by destitution,

fear too naked for her own shadow's shape?
In 1944, an Alsatian who composed

poems in French and in German, exiled
for fear of death in a state-created camp—

his eye structure, by law, defined as "Jewish"—
sensed the gist. Diagnosed with leukemia,

Yvan Goll gave the name Lackawanna
Mannahatta to our metropolis—Mannahatta

locked in Judgment's pregnant days, he sang,
Lackawanna of pregnant nights and sulfurous

pheasant mortality riddled with light
lying dormant in a shock of blond hair

half made of telephones, half made of tears.
The heavy changes of the light—I know.

Faint sliver of new moon and distant Mars
glow through to Lackawanna Mannahatta.

Above a street in the lower Nineties
several leaves from an old ginkgo tree

twist through blackish red on golden air
outside a fashionable bistro where a man

with medals worn across a tailor-cut suit
chides a becoming woman half his age.

"From now on, my dear," he says with authority,
"from now on it's every man for himself."

MOVEMENT IN THE DISTANCE IS LARGER UP CLOSE

Apart from that, the sun came around
the same time. A certain splendor emerged
illusory and frail, like a rainbow.
Around where we were standing everything
suffused apricot brightness. Even the man
alone in the Café Fledermaus, his table
covered by an old salmon-pink *Financial Times*,
feels he's metering his thoughts, gesturing
as if speaking. These curved lines,

so many images, but it's necessary to observe again
the rest of it split, one part like money, forever within
the daily routine, another mixing fragments
of harmonic nuances abstract and grounded by the beat,
under the influence of connoisseurs of rhythm, not
afraid of being blue, brain on fire from time to time,
longing intensified to the point of—yes. I hear
you. Your absence more palpable than your presence.
And me? I'm often short of breath these days.
But, then, so are the philosophers, whose problems are
the politicians' now. That man on television, for example,
the head of state who bunches his nails onto his lips,
throwing them outward as if under the pressure of some invisible
bouquet magically forced out of his mouth, clacking his tongue,
proclaiming the inevitability between Kazakhstan and Sudan;
and there are many new Americas to discover.

I don't know about you, but it all goes through my skin.
Like the woman over there coughing into the pay phone.
Enlightenment? I've got mine, you've got yours—then what?
I know a prophet who possesses the power of thought transference,
addresses women mostly, recently seen carrying an olive branch.
But can't you see eventually we will be forced to acknowledge
countless children possess an alien language, face it,

get down! The hype alone's no beautiful thing.
What's sold: used shoes to those who prove
indigency. Hot and spicy pork for the ego.
Vodka for pleasure, votive candles to the Virgin.
What's bought: this displaced child, hugging
a kneeling woman, about to ascend into limbo.
So you rampage within yourself—you think
you should be thanked for it? In history's optic
movement in the distance is larger up close. This is
no proverb. Of course I remember that day, the leaves
a deep, irascible mauve, boundless happiness and joy.
Precisely; where we ought to be.

NOW EVENING COMES FAST FROM THE SEA

The East River looks as black
as the Brooklyn Bridge's shadow.

Thinking back—but those days
are over! A darkening green

conceals the Heights, quivering
twilight cold. I can't

be alone. And yet, somehow
or other, in spite,

or because of you transposed
in the treble of light

that lingers where the music
remains, a great and nuanced

diamond sheet projects itself
at the end of the street,

against the sky. So, still,
refracted into depths,

all beauty isn't underlined;
indignant and ironic

events blocked on top of one another,
dislocations debited

to anamorphosized tribes, city
drawn, caressed, into

circles—do you follow me?
Now evening comes fast from the sea.

OCCIDENT—ORIENT EXPRESS

East and west, converged expression,
analytical instincts, erupted harmonies:
all night a blind woman listens alone
to the radio. And in Tokyo Madame Lenine's
grandniece eats air-blown tuna
pungent as caviar. What do I mean?
Language means. And Jerusalem
hangs mystical in lavender sky
while outside Bethlehem the prophet Elijah is seen
entering a UFO.

Straining to catch the light again,
colorless light, bunches of violets,
a proud, shy woman silently sipping tea.
The process of logical association
you can't escape: the taxi driver
flashes his teeth, "It's in the eyes,
you have to break the other's eyes."
But if you love to hear a heartbeat
you won't sleep too well alone. At noon
parts of the world are black with sun.

Or this rumor out of Lebanon:
Party of God regulars taught to kill
by Vietnam War veterans from Las Vegas.
The People's Republic programmatically

nullifies half its language.
The Isle of Dogs's rumor the Prime Minister's
capillaries quickened daily
by doses of electricity
—reservoirs of the impulse to work something out
every place.

Or this: Moscow, coveting cash, visits Bonn.
Before the bust of Adenauer on the Rhine
a vista appears in the Chairman's mind:
a bright nation cleft with roses
swaying in yellow and flame.
"Where there's a will
there's a way," he assures his bankers
in English, almost singing;
a priapism of form everyone present
giggles at.

Against my heart I listen to you
all the time, all the time.
Against my brain, more visible than dream,
the present's elongations spread
blue behind the fragrant curves
pure abstractions blast through
a fragile mind in a flapping coat
descending the Memorial's steps
toward incalculable rays of sun
set perpendicular into the earth.

Into It

(2005)

IN IT, INTO IT, INSIDE IT, DOWN IN

How far to go?—I have to, I know,
I promised. But how? How, and when?

And where? It was cold. The sky,
blue, almost burst, leaves burnished

yellow. Nearing Liberty, Liberty
and Church streets. So it happened

in early November. Which is to say
a story took place. Once again

new lines, new colors. One scene
and then another. Characters talking

to one another. It was she who
opened the conversation. "A wild rose,

and grapes on vines along the ground,
a butterfly on the green palmetto,

plums the size of walnuts, gray
and vermillion"—she sat up straighter,

lips pressed together, looking me
square in the eyes—"and why, you tell me why,

in this time of so many claims to morality,
the weight of violence

is unparalleled in the history
of the species ..." What needs to be said—

why not say it? "Who dares to learn
what concerns him intimately,"

is how he says it in his book. Then the mind
runs through the spaces left behind, crossing

over to a different place. It certainly was
a well-dressed crowd. Here, again, the General,

the Attorney General, a beeper in one hand,
a crucifix in the other; here, again,

language, a language—a style, a groove, a fate.
On the esplanade, Battery Park, a newspaper,

old, caught in a gust, a child,
lost, crying—the pain was ours, I know it now;

beauty, the answer, if you must know—
the sun ablaze on the harbor. Hearing

a sentence phrased in ... a tenor? countertenor? ...
an error of nature, after all—made

of thought and of sound, of feelings seen—
in it, into it, inside it, down in.

WHEN ONE IS FEELING ONE'S WAY

I

The sky was red and the earth got hot,
like a hundred degrees hot, I mean.
"Stay cool," the monk was said to have said,
"you've still got a long way to go."
A monk, say, of Hue, who, to protest
the killing of innocents, is dragging
an altar on—yes it was, Hillside Avenue.
So what else is new? One new
voice mail message. A woman,
a certain woman, has been seen, eyes,
liquid blue eyes, glistening with tears.

II

Two things, the two things that are interesting
are history and grammar.
In among the foundations of the intelligence
the chemistries of words. "The fault lines
of risk concealed in a monetary landscape . . ."
What of it? Nothing but the same resistance
since the time of the Gracchi—
against the arrogation by private interests
of the common wealth,

against the precious and the turgid language
of pseudoerudition (thugs,
thugs are what they are,
false-voiced God-talkers and power freaks
who think not at all about what they bring down).

III

A pause. Any evening, every evening.
When one is feeling one's way
the pattern is small and complex.
At center a moral issue, but composed,
and first. Looks to me like,
across the train yards, a blurred sun
setting behind the high ground
on the other side of the Hudson,
overhead purple and pink.
A changing set of marginal options.
Whole lots of amplified light.

IV

Oh, I get the idea. That image,
the focal point
of a concave mirror, is old.

And that which is unintermitted
and fragile, wild and fragile (there,
behind the freighter's yellow
puffs of smoke; God, no, I haven't
forgotten it) is, I said,
still fragile, still proud.

I NOTE IN A NOTEBOOK

Pink sunlight, blue sky, snowed-upon January morning.
The romantic restated—a woman and a man
by themselves, each alone in the other. Those
transcriptions of the inexpressible—perhaps
the experience of having heaven
is just simply perfect luck … That winter,
on Belle Isle, the ice floes, the Seven Sister
smokestacks. In Angel Park, a figure in motion,
muted reds and grays, clouds and light, and shadows
in motion, a freezing wind out of Canada
over the lake. A figure, in the factory
behind the Jefferson Avenue Assembly, marking
and filing the parts of the new model prototype
Chryslers, standing at a window, smoking a Kool.
Those with the masks of hyenas are the bosses,
and those wearing mass-produced shirts and pants,
among them my father … Cavafy's poem, the one
about how if he's wasted his life in this corner
of the world he's wasted it everywhere. What
is happening, what is done. Convicted
of rape and murder, he leaves a piece of pie
in his cell, believing he'll be able to eat it
after he's electrocuted—the fact that a compound,
1,3-diphenyl propane, forged from the fires'
heat and pressure, combined with the Towers'
collapse, has never been seen before.

The technology to abolish truth is now available—
not everyone can afford it, but it is available—
when the cost comes down, as it will, then what?
Pasolini's desire to make, to write, an intricate,
yet rational mosaic, byzantine and worth, at least,
a second, or even a third, reading . . . An epical
turn, so great a turn—her voice in him,
his voice in her—the vista, a city,
the city, taking a shape and burning . . .

INCLINED TO SPEAK

I saw that. One woman, her personality
and appearance described as lovely,
while performing her predawn prayers,
watched the attackers shoot to death her husband,
her seven-year-old son, three of her brothers,
as they grabbed her four-year-old son from her arms
and cut his throat, taking her and her two sisters
away on horses and raping them. Of course it's genocide.
And, yes, it brings to mind I am constantly aware of,
in making the poem, Brecht's point, to write about trees—
implicitly, too, to write about pleasure—
in times of killing like these, is a crime;
and Paul Celan's response, that for Brecht a leaf
is a leaf without a tree, that what kinds of times
are these when a conversation—Celan believed a poem
is a conversation—what kinds of times are these
when a poem is a crime because it includes
what must be made explicit.

What is seen, heard, and imagined
at the same time—that truth. A sort of relationship
is established between our attention
to what is furthest from us
and what deepest in us. The immense enlargement
of our perspectives is confronted
by a reduction in our powers of action, which reduces
a voice to an inner voice inclined to speak only
to those closest to us . . .

THE PATTERN-PARALLEL MAP OR GRAPH

The sky?—ultramarine, tinted black, lines
of black ink. Newspapers, mud, fishtails,
betel nuts, trampled on along Canal Street.

Luck turns out hot. According to the story
taken from Apuleius, Eros's and Psyche's
bodies are wet and hot.

                    Nine years—
where does that take us on the pattern-parallel
map or graph? Nine years from two thousand—
nineteen ninety-one … Wallace Stevens—him again—
in his commonplace book,
an entry made in nineteen thirty-four:
"Ananke is necessity or fate personified:
the saeva Necessitas of Horace
Odes Book I No. 35, to Fortune."

I am among those who hear it. Chromatically
suspended, the notes feeling their way from intervals
to motifs, a progression in a manner that disguises
the key—a linear polyphony forming harmonies
in strange developments, all kinds of different stuff,
mixed and fused, chunks of vibrato. Simultaneity requires
the use of a topological logic. Time compressed—interactivity
escalated to maximum speed. Why not just change
their official status from human to animal, they're forced
to live like animals already—once they've attained animal status,

then dozens of groups will come forward to defend them.
What, in let's say twelve years, will the zone of suffering
outside the established orders look like? There is Venus
moving across the sun in a mini-eclipse visible twice
every century. There is a God, an achieved conception,
accessible and inaccessible, merciful and just, human
and divine, completed not far from the Black Sea.
That mood, intensely subjective, scenes and myths
reemerged. There, on the table, is a flower the yellow
of flax, irises unfolding, another deep blue-purple,
a third larger and china blue. There, a small, bright
red bird in a wooden cage in a store on East Broadway,
illuminated scrolls unrolled on the counter . . .

WOODWARD AVENUE

The destination, the destiny, a street,
an avenue. When General MacArthur, deviating
from his itinerary, was driven out
to the Shrine at Twelve Mile Road
and Woodward to help in Coughlin's
rehabilitation. History followed
in the direction of a more or a less
cosmological evolution. On the ground
the authorities began to sense the situation
was going to get worse before it got better.
Around midnight the street was blocked,
a man, backed up against a white
Mustang, was beaten. What was it like?
The essential principles were power,
accuracy, economy, system, and speed.
The Highland Park plant was known
as the Crystal Palace because of its expanse
of windows. Moving assembly lines, conveyor
belts, gravity feeds, and railroads
constituted the materials-handling
network, portrayed, metaphorically, as a wave
of production. No singularities.
In Paperbacks Unlimited, an essay,
"The Law of Love and the Law of Violence,"
in a book of pamphlets and essays by Tolstoy.
The struggle for the "imperium mundi" down to

a not so sudden sorrow. My father
listens to the radio, reading. The past
rearranged by hardening arteries.
My grandfather's voice doesn't leave me.
So many voices, which of them to be taken
seriously? Am I mistaken or was napalm
transported by teamsters from Midland?
Am I not correct in saying that for purposes
of insurance there was considerable dispute
as to whether it was a war, a riot,
or an insurrection? An arm's snapped,
a body's kicked down darkened stairs,
a face is spit into, one of the babies
is left to die. The Greek dictionary
lies on the kitchen table. There's a torn
photograph of the Blessed Sacrament
grade school basketball team, and, here,
a ticket stub from the championship game
held in the Memorial Building. Screaming
all day about war. Screaming that nothing
can be solved. Only the very poorest spirits
can't be roused by the practical, where we
literally are, approach. Remember that?
The heavyweight champion of the world, found
in a stupor without his false teeth, naked
in the backseat of his Continental convertible
in the parking lot of The Last Chance Bar.
Neither the proclamation nor the plea
had any effect. The men of the 701st

Military Police Battalion in full battle gear,
bayonets fixed at high port, moving through
Cadillac Square to disperse the mob of over
ten thousand. He was, Henry Ford said,
not in the business of making cars
but in the business of making money.
The Algiers Motel? U-shaped, with neon lights,
swimming pool lined by a metal fence
and faded beach umbrellas, the style
Florida Gulf Port traditional, set
back from the street, a rusted Carte Blanche
sign swinging on a post out front
Reality explained. Those corners where
the little one curled up and went to sleep
when she was tired, where, when she was
unsure of herself, she secretly went to cry.
I can smell something cooking—I can tell
there's going to be a feast. A thickish
film sticks to the windshields and the lungs,
dawn is burnt red along the landscape's rim.
Smoke that sketches the sky with gray.
Gray. Smoke-gray. The mist lifts.
So drive this street and drop into
this hell where a man was once cut
from ear to ear. High winds again,
an unexpected chill. A soft, misty rain.
Patches of pavement oiled and streaked
with rain. The appointed time, in detail—
the crazy weave of the perfect mind.

How much later, the light snow lay encrusted
on the oak leaves until the wind turned
a leaf over. The wind blowing constantly.
Can you get to it? A dance that you get to,
"The Double-Clutch." Listen. Sure is funky.
Everyone clapping their hands, popping
their fingers, everyone hip, has walks.
Effects are supplied, both rhythmic
and textual. Another take? Same key?
Sometimes you've just got to improvise a bit
before you're in a groove. Listen.
That's right. It's an illumination.
That which occurs in authentic light.
Like the man said. So many selves—
the one who detects the sound of a voice,
that voice—the voice that compounds
his voice—that self obedient to that fate,
increased, enlarged, transparent, changing.

WHY NOT SAY WHAT HAPPENS?

I

Of icons. Of divination. Of Gods. Repetitions
without end. I have it in my notes,
a translation from the Latin, a commentary
on the Book of Revelation—"the greater
the concentration of power on earth,
the more truth is stripped of its power,
the holiest innocent, in eternity,
is 'as though slain.'"
It has nothing to do with the apocalyptic.
The seven-headed beast from the sea,
the two-horned beast from the earth, have always—
I know, I've studied it—been with us.
Me? I'm only an accessory to particular images.

II

According to the translation of the police transcript,
the sheikh—the arrested head
of the cell mockingly said—in a plot
involving a chemical attack,
needs, simply,
two or three young men with brains and training
with nothing to gain or lose,

not an army.
It doesn't take much these days to be a prophet.
Do you know how much poison can be put
in a ten-liter barrel?
You pour it and spread it, then you leave.
The web is, prosecutors believe,
so intricate, the detainee,
they think, may also be a member
of cells in Barcelona and Frankfurt.

III

Yet another latest version of another
ancient practice—mercenaries, as they were once known,
are thriving, only this time
they're called "private military contractors."
During the last few years their employees
have been sent to Bosnia, Nigeria, Colombia, and, of course,
most recently, Iraq. No one knows
how extensive the industry is, but some military experts
estimate a market of tens of billions of dollars.

IV

Autumn turned to winter and the site
began to clear. The limits of my language
are the limits of my world, said Wittgenstein.

The realization—the state of the physical world
depends on shifts in the delusional thinking
of very small groups. One of Garfinkle's patients
tripped over a severed foot while evacuating
the Stock Exchange. Several others saw
the first plane pass right next to the almost
floor-length windows of their conference room.
"When I'm not working, the last thing I want to do
is talk about it," said one policeman, who,
like many of the city's uniformed officers,
is still working a schedule of twelve hours on,
twelve hours off... Shoes, books, wallets, jewelry,
watches, some of them still keeping time...
The congressman says he can't say for sure
there isn't a suitcase with a nuclear bomb
floating around out there. Everything
immense and out of context. The large item
in the mud, one of the motors that powered
the Towers' elevators. "It's intense"—
says Lieutenant Bovine—"no photographs! This is
a crime scene!" What happened was one floor
fell on top of another, as many as ten floors
compressed into a foot of space. What fell
was mostly metal... The cement vaporized...
The Night Watch was what the laid-out scene
looked like. The fences around the wreckage
covered with T-shirts, teddy bears, and memorial
banners signed by thousands of visitors;
tourists snap pictures, and, subject to the way

the wind is blowing, the air is tinged
with an acrid smoke ... "Lost/Missing Family
1-866-856-4167 or 1-212-741-4626 ..." A Web Exclusive,
the poet will speak about poetry and grief ...
The smells of burning wiring, dankness
from the tunnels, the sharp and sweet
cherrylike smell of death. At eight-ten on Friday
two more bodies are found in a stairwell
of the South Tower. Work, again, stops,
and the ironworkers, who have been cutting
steel beams, come out from the hole. The work
goes on until well past midnight. More debris
is removed, another body recovered. A group
of ironworkers stands on a gnarled beam,
one end of which juts over the pit
like a gangplank. Three 35-millimeter movie cameras
are placed on top of nearby buildings, each programmed
to take a picture every five minutes, day and night.
A bugler slips onto the site and plays "Taps."

V

That period of ten or eleven years—
concerning it I can express myself briefly.
At some point, in collective time, electronic space
turned into time. The miraculous
multiplication of loaves was restricted to the rentiers.
A grappa in a black, pyramid-shaped bottle

was taken cognizance of,
and, with no resistance,
for the most part, no guarantees
were made for the slow, the meek, or the poor of spirit,
who, for reasons unexplained,
allowed themselves to disappear
into the long, red evenings, night's early gray-blues.

VI

Screaming—those who could
sprinting—south toward
Battery Park, the dark cloud
funneling slowly—
there are two things you should know
about this cloud—
one, it isn't only ash and soot
but metal, glass, concrete, and flesh,
and, two, soon
any one of these pieces
of metal, glass, or concrete
might go through you.
As she turns to run, a woman's bag
comes off her shoulder,
bright silver compact discs sent
spinning along the ground, a man,
older, to the right,
is tripping,

falls against the pavement,
glasses flying
off his face.

VII

Have I mentioned my grandmother,
my father's mother, who died long ago
but who visits me in dreams?
It's to her, mostly, I owe
the feeling that, in cases of need,
those transfigured in eternal love help us
certainly with eternal,
and, perhaps, also, with temporal gifts;
that, in eternal love, all is gratis—
all that comes from eternal love
is gratis.

VIII

My father?—my father was a worker. I can still hear him
getting up in the morning to go to work.
Sadness, too, has to be learned,
and it took my father time to learn it,
but he did, though when he did
his tears were never chronic.

As for the economies on which my parents' lives depended,
they won't be found
in any book.

IX

It's the details that dream out
the plot. Rearrange the lies, the conceits,
the crimes, the exploitation
of needs and desires,
and it's still there, the whole system's
nervous system—inside it,
at times, a dreamer at work, right now
it's me. The air not yet too cold with winter,
at a sidewalk table at the Cornelia Street Café—
a dream, it's a dream, the dream
of a dream song, the dream of a dream,
a glass of Sancerre on the table, re-visioning,
in a purple mist, a tugboat, practical and hard,
as it approaches a freighter,
black, with the red-lettered name BYZANTIUM.

X

Capital? Careful! Capital capitalizes,
assimilates, makes

its own substance, revitalizing
its being, a vast metabolism absorbing even
the most ancient exchanges, running away,
as the cyberneticians put it,
performing, as it does, its own
anthropomorphosis, its triumph
the triumph of mediation—
and, let's not forget,
it organizes, capital organizes, capital is
"an organizing,"
organizing
social forms.

XI

Pink above the Hudson
against the shadows lingering still,
the sky above an even blue and changing
to a pale gray and rose.
A coat of snow in the park on Tenth Avenue,
clumps of grass sticking
out of it, late afternoon, in Druids,
Sam Cooke on the jukebox, lines
from an obscure tune from the box set,
"even my voice belongs to you,
I use my voice to sing, to sing, to sing to you . . ."
The lives of the two or three others who pass through
as close to you as the weather.

Walking back, the dotted lines
of the lights on the Bridge, the sun
blotted out by a burst of vermilion.

XII

I remember it—the gold burnt into gold,
the gold on gold and on white and yellow,
an incandescence condensing the sunlight,
outburning the sunlight, the factory
molten, the sun behind it, in it, thin,
gold, pig iron, a spray of fire, flywheels
revolving through the floor, rims almost
reaching the roof, enormous engines
throwing great pounding cylindrical arms
back and forth, as if the machines
are playing a game, trying to see how much
momentum can be withstood before one
or the other gives way. I remember—down Sixth
to Downing, to Varick, down Varick, downtown.
A cat is in the rubbish in the street. The sun
over Jersey. The gap at the end of West Street,
the sun on the clock tower. The melancholy
induced by the pressure of time, the wavering
ambitions, failed ideas, time wasted.
The unexpected breeze, warm, the sense
of the river. The sky blue, dark blue
yet pure in color, not blackened

or tarnished, above the low, old
buildings, like a painting of something
solid rather than the solid thing itself,
a high and low composition. But what
light there is in that landscape . . .

IN A MOOD

Less stupid than I seem, less
intelligent than I think. Observing

the subtlety innately a part of Near
Eastern manners, the mysterious

uses of power not entrusted to me.
Holy books' tribal signs inscribed

on skulls, a war—the Undersecretary
for Imperial Affairs says with a shrug—

is a lot more than a cosmic phenomenon.
In the spaciousness of syntax and text,

history's, or a history's, spaces composed,
the feeling, the meaning, aspired to,

the poem of an era. What will, indeed,
be revealed by the most expert lies

binds which economy, which comedy?
And all those memories in a mood.

Lilac-shaded shades of dark green
around the Bridge—that too, that evening.

A woman and a man beside the river . . .
A line consisting of a burning sky,

a sky on fire . . . the sky is on fire!
Then what, and then again what, unfolded . . .

UNYIELDINGLY PRESENT

Near the curb beside the police lines
a pool of blood, the gas tanks of the cars

in the garage on West Street
exploding, an air tank, its out-of-air

alarm going off, pops, and is skidding.
That woman staring into space, her dress

on fire. What transpires in
a second. On an intact floor

a globe of the world
bursts like a balloon. A ceiling-mounted

exit sign is melting. Facile equivalences
are to be avoided. Hell the horrific

into the routine. Glass and metal
can be identified, not the atoms

of human ash. I set down thoughts. Sequences
of images, of emotions, dissolved

in a mass, encoded in the brain.
The depth or the width of the hatred measured?

From so high up the time it takes for those
who are falling. Is it that reality, disjointed,

cannot be discerned, or that consciousness,
disjointed, cannot discern it?

The message I am communicating,
this beam of focused energy, no, I said,

no, I am not going to allow anything
to happen to you. I summon up

in my mind a place where my thoughts will find
yours—no, nothing is going to happen to you.

An issue of language now,
isn't it? There are these vicious circles

of accumulated causation.
Irreal is the word. I know of no

defense against those addicted to death. God.
My God. I thought it was over, absolutely

had to be. What am I supposed to feel?
Images that, after that, loop in the head.

Looming ahead, in the smoke, that man
at the railing can't breathe.

I'm having trouble breathing, he says.
You saw it? I saw it. I'm frightened.

This is about—which states of mind? Solid brown
and gray, a muddy mass of debris,

of powder. There is a strip of window glazing
hanging from—what kind of a tree?

What isn't separated, what isn't
scribbled, what will not be metamorphosed,

reduced, occurring, it will be said,
unyieldingly fixed, unyieldingly present . . .

NEWS BACK EVEN FURTHER THAN THAT

I

Dust, the dust of a dust storm;
yellow, black, brown, haze, smoke;
a baby photographed with half
a head; the stolen Thoroughbred
a boy is riding bareback attacked
by a lion; the palace, fixed up
as a forward command post—"This,"
says Air-War Commander Mosely,
"would make a pretty nice casino";
why is such a detailed
description necessary?
that smell in the air is the smell
of burned human flesh;
those low-flying A-10 Warthogs
are, each of them, firing
one hundred bullets a second.

II

The President refuses to answer a question
he wasn't asked. The President denies
his eyes are the eyes of a lobster.
The map is being drawn: Mosul in the north,

Baghdad in the center, Basra in the south.
The news back even further than that:
"He Says He Is the Prophet Ezekiel.
In the Great Mudflats by the River Chebar,
He Has Seen, He Proclaims, Four Angels,
Each with Six Wings, on a Fiery Wheel."
Collaborators cut into pieces and burnt to death
in public, on spits, like lambs. In spray paint
across the armored personnel carrier:
"Crazy Train," "Rebel," "Got Oil?" There,
on Sadoun Street, in a wheelbarrow, a coil
of wire, a carpet, rolled, Persian, antique.

III

"I've just been to see her. It's made her
mad—angry, yes, of course, but I mean mad,
truly mad. She spoke quietly, quickly—
maniacally. 'Wargame, they're using wargame
as a verb, they didn't wargame the chaos—
chaos! Do you think they care about
the chaos? The chaos just makes it easier for them
to get what they want. Wargame!
What they've wargamed is the oil,
their possession of the oil, what they've wargamed
is the killing, the destruction,
what they've wargamed is their greed . . .'
Had I noticed that Lebanon had become

an abstract noun, as in 'the Lebanonization of'?
'It may just as well have been two or three
atomic bombs, the amount of depleted
uranium in their bombs, the bombs
in this war, the bombs in the war before this—
uranium's in the groundwater now,
uranium is throughout the entire
ecology by now, how many generations
are going to be
contaminated by it, die of it, be poisoned by it?'
War, a war time, without limits.
Technocapital war a part
of our bodies, of the body politic.
She quoted Pound—the *Pisan Cantos*—
she couldn't remember which—
there are no righteous wars.
'There is no righteous violence,'
she said, 'it's neurobiological
with people like this—
people who need to destroy and who need to kill
like this—and what we're seeing now
is nothing compared
to what we'll see in the future . . .' "

THE SINGLE NECESSITY

Those days eternities went through everything.
The extraneous—
that which is not experienced and imagined
in detail.
I observed a loose strand of her hair on her forehead
and loved her even more.

HISTORY FOR ANOTHER TIME

It was, of course,
impossible to have predicted the economic
cycle had peaked, perhaps the most . . .
what's the word? remarkable?—
perhaps the most remarkable period
in the history of capitalism. A little over
a three-hundred-seventeen-point drop in the Dow
in one day, only a few points' recovery the day after that.
Here was an item—forty-five-ish,
tall, with wire-frame glasses,
curly gray hair, his background
is in cable. He says
he has his visions. HorizontalNet
establishes separate Web sites
or horizontal portals—hortals he calls them—
for the waste management industry. Incidentally,
he wonders, do I have any idea how easy it is
to convert a digital watch into a timer?—
that all you've got to do is use
lightbulb filaments to ignite cotton
soaked in nitrocellulose, and you've got yourself
a detonated bomb.

        Look, it's on the record.
When asked to explain a personal motive
he may have had for the war, the President

unzipped his fly, took out his quite sizable member,
and replied, "Motive? You want my personal motive?
My personal motive is right here."
A massacre of eight hundred thousand
during the last hundred days is reported.
A rumor the rat is the newest unit of currency.
A skull, a child's shoe, stick out of the rubble in a room
on the church grounds where the dead
number over ten thousand. Rain-soaked mattresses,
lampshades, rotting piles of clothing
in heaps inside artillery-shelled houses.
Rats, I think I said, are being considered
as the unit of currency by the new government.

Pressure is what
it's about, and pressure's incalculable—
which eludes the historian. For a charge
of ten percent above the official rates,
weapons of every caliber can be supplied
from any country, be it North or South American,
Asian, or European. The whole world sells arms
through this consortium. Implements for killing
are among the most lucrative of commodities.
Supposedly, he and his son, and his son's
associates, have a sort of de facto monopoly
on the banana trade with Iran, linking his family
with the present occupants of the Baabda Palace.
That disturbance had no clear perimeter.
While some streets appeared safer than others,

there really was nowhere to hide. By midday
bands of looters were moving in waves
toward the small strip of shopping centers.
At one point men and women on the street
screamed, a red, seventies-vintage Cadillac
careened down the boulevard, its occupants
sitting on the edges of opened car windows
brandishing axes, the sky still bright at this end
of the city, the smoke and the sirens miles away,
at least for the time being. It is—it always is—
beginning again. It's unreal, the extent to which
all political discourse is the same. Legal relations
arising out of economic relations—Engels, isn't it?
I can't remember where I read it. Let me see
if I can remember. These days it's child's play
to figure out how things worked, as Brecht did—
in phase one, competitive capital,
or phase two, imperialism—to find the metaphors
to express it. Each phase had its machines
(in phase one, steam-driven motors, electric
or combustion motors in phase two) and its critical
structure (realism in the first phase, modernism
in the second).The present phase,
with its electronic and its nuclear-powered motors—
the era of after, or postmodernism—has proven
more difficult to configure. Its characteristic
machine, the computer, contains no emblematic
power. You can no more describe the heart
of a computer than the heart of a multinational

corporation. What's at the heart of a global
network of microcircuits? What is ancient
isn't what is chronologically the oldest
but that which emerges from the innermost
laws of time. Imagining how the universe
made its "quantum leap from eternity into time."
The universe bringing itself into being
by the accumulation of trillions upon trillions
of quantum interactions, the universe,
microscopically, forced by itself into being,
the consequence of which is that the past has no existence
except in the present. If the creation
of the universe happens outside time,
it must happen all the time, the big bang
here and now, the foundation of every instant . . .
The sudden breaking and tearing of space . . .
That ancient story, how they, in the combining
of their forms, in the necessity and logic
of purest form, in the logic of a dream—
the dimensions are inverted, and that place,
immense, is small now, the two of them
a dot on the red horizon. Neither seriousness
nor laughter is much help, either. You need only
be approached by one of the beggars
in Pennsylvania Station to see that certain rules
prevail in our midst. Still I,
for one, don't condone cut-off ears . . .

THAT TOO

A long walk up West Street along the piers.
The sky—right now the sun,
the clouds, a few seconds of light yellow.

The deepest being being a longing
to satisfy the longing for a solitude of two.

Gertrude Stein's "Composition as Explanation," that too.

Surely the blacks and golds
are the depth of a late October afternoon. Surely
the blues and greens fired by crimson are the sea.

THE GAME CHANGED

The phantasmic imperium is set in a chronic
state of hypnotic fixity. I have absolutely
no idea what the fuck you're talking about
was his reply, and he wasn't laughing,
either, one of the most repellent human beings
I've ever known, his presence a gross and slippery
lie, a piece of chemically pure evil. A lawyer—
although the type's not exclusive to lawyers.
A lot of different minds touch, and have touched,
the blood money in the dummy account
in an offshore bank, washed clean, free to be
transferred into a hedge fund or a foreign
brokerage account, at least half a trillion
ending up in the United States, with more to come.
I believe I told you I'm a lawyer. Which has had
little or no effect on a certain respect
I have for occurrences that suggest laws
of necessity. I too am thinking of it
as a journey—the journey with conversations
otherwise known as the *Divina Commedia*
is how Osip Mandelstam characterized Dante's poem.
Lebanon? I hear the Maronite Patriarch
dares the Syrians to kill him, no word
from my grandfather's side of the family
in the Shouf. "There are circles here"—
to quote the professor of international

relations and anthropology—"Vietnam, Lebanon,
and Iraq . . . Hanoi, Beirut, and Baghdad."
The beggar in Rome is the beggar in Istanbul,
the blind beggar is playing saxophone,
his legs covered with a zebra-striped blanket,
the woman beside him holding an aluminum cup,
beside them, out of a shopping bag, the eyes
of a small, sick dog. I'm no pseudoaesthete.
It's a physical thing. An enthusiasm,
a transport. The melancholy is ancient.
The intent is to make a large, serious
portrait of my time. The sun on the market
near Bowling Green, something red, something
purple, bunches of roses and lilacs. A local
issue for those of us in the neighborhood.
Not to know what it is you're breathing
in a week when Black Hawk helicopters resume
patrolling the harbor. Two young men
blow themselves up attaching explosives
on the back of a cat. An insurgency:
commandos are employed, capital is manipulated
to secure the oil of the Asian Republics.
I was walking in the Forties when I saw it—
a billboard with a background of brilliant
blue sky, with writing on it in soft-edged,
irregularly spaced, airy-white letters
already drifting off into the air, as if they'd
been sky-written—"The World Really Does
Revolve Around You." The taxi driver rushes

to reach his family before the camp is closed—
"There is no way I will leave, there is no way—
they will have to kill us, and, even if
they kill every one of us, we won't leave." Sweat
dripping from her brow, she picks up the shattered,
charred bones. She works for the Commission
on Missing Persons. "First they kill them,"
she says, "then they burn them, then they cover them
with dead babies . . ." Neither impenetrable opacity
nor absolute transparency. I know what I'm after.
The entire poem is finished in my head. No,
I mean the entire poem. The color, the graphic
parts, the placement of solid bodies in space,
gradations of light and dark, the arrangements
of pictorial elements on a single plane
without a loss of depth. This habit of wishing—
as if one's mother and father lay in one's heart
and wished as they had always wished—that voice,
one of the great voices, worth listening to.
A continuity in which everything is transition.
To repeat it because it's worth repeating. Immanence—
an immanence and a happiness. Yes, exquisite—
an exquisite dream. The mind on fire
possessed by what is desired—the game changed.

ONCE AGAIN

The esplanade. High summer.
The sea is beyond

the sunset's light—
the shapes amassed, the sky

a current carrying us along,
heavy with that green and that black.

Fate's precisive wheel revolving,
force's writhing wheel—

the stealing, the killing, accomplished
by new types of half-monsters—

it's what I said—
the poem is the dream, a dream technique;

the primary soul-substance
on which our attention is fixed—

supernal, metaphysical—in other words,
a representation,

as we have seen,
of mythical origins.

Something felt, something needed—
as much as we needed;

a woman, a man,
love's characters, the myth

their own. We are agreed.
The moon is low, its silent flame

across the garden of roses, almost level
with the harbor. We place our hands

on the silence
and, once again, repeat the vow.

So Where Are We?

(2017)

A FABLE

Great bronze doors of Trinity Church, hours
told by the sounds of bells. A red

tugboat pushes a red and gold barge
into the Narrows. A bench in the shadows

on a pier in the Hudson. The café
on Cornelia Street, the music,

now whose voice might that be? Diffuse,
invisible, energy. The flow of data

since the attacks has surged.
Technocapital, permanently, digitally,

semioticized, virtually unlimited
in freedom and power, taking

billions of bodies on the planet
with it. Future, past, cosmogonies,

the void, are in whose vision?
Ever-deepening, ravenous

cruelty, viciousness, annihilation,
defended and worshipped.

But is there a more beautiful city—parts
of it, anyway? Another path to the harbor,

the border between sea and land
fluctuating, a line, a curve. Peck Slip

to Water Street to Front Street
to Pine, to Coenties Slip to Pearl

to Stone Street to Exchange Place,
the light in majestic degrees.

This is a fable. A final nail
driven in. The Recording Angel

completes the exactest chronicle.
Blake, with blazing eyes, loves

issues of eternal time. Gauguin
puts a final green on the canvas

of the *Self-Portrait with Yellow
Christ*, to complicate the idea.

SO WHERE ARE WE?

So where were we? The fiery
avalanche headed right at us—falling,

flailing bodies in midair—
the neighborhood under thick gray powder—

on every screen. I don't know
where you are, I don't know what

I'm going to do, I heard a man say;
the man who had spoken was myself.

What year? Which Southwest Asian war?
Smoke from infants' brains

on fire from the phosphorus
hours after they're killed, killers

reveling in the horror. The more obscene
the better. The point at which

a hundred thousand massacred
is just a detail. Asset and credit bubbles

about to burst. Too much consciousness
of too much at once, a tangle of tenses

and parallel thoughts, a series of feelings
overlapping a sudden sensation

felt and known, those chains of small facts
repeated endlessly, in the depths

of silent time. So where are we?
My ear turns, like an animal's. I listen.

Like it or not, a digital you is out there.
Half of that city's buildings aren't there.

Who was there when something was, and a witness
to it? The rich boy general conducts the Pakistani

heroin trade on a satellite phone from his cave.
On the top floor of the Federal Reserve

in an office looking onto Liberty
at the South Tower's onetime space,

the Secretary of the Treasury concedes
they got killed in terms of perceptions.

Ten blocks away the Church of the Transfiguration,
in the back a Byzantine Madonna—

there is a God, a God who fits the drama
in a very particular sense. What you said—

the memory of a memory of a remembered
memory, the color of a memory, violet and black.

The lunar eclipse on the winter solstice,
the moon a red and black and copper hue.

The streets, the harbor, the light, the sky.
The blue and cloudless intense and blue morning sky.

IN A POST-BUBBLE CREDIT-COLLAPSE ENVIRONMENT

No clouds, now, nearer to Brooklyn Bridge
than the Bridge is to the Heights. Half a block east,

barefoot on shards of glass, a towel wrapped
around his waist, shaving cream on the left side

of his face—a block south, beside a fire hydrant,
a leg found severed at the knee. Internal or external—

what difference does it make? I shake the snow
from my coat, take off my gloves, set them

on the counter. I step back onto Spring Street,
and, on Greenwich, start downtown. Sight and sound

reconfigured, details, truths, colors, and shapes
round out the aesthetic. Things changed

and unchanged, not just in abstract ways.
This young man, yellow pants, undershirt,

stands eating from a garbage bin, patches of ice
on the East River esplanade. One World

Trade Center's structural steel has reached
the fifty-second of a hundred and four stories.

The light in a pink and a coral, moving through
pink and violet scumbled over pink, turning red

on violet. That was yesterday's twilight—this afternoon
white and gray, and hot. Is everything between

six banks and everything else connected, does the old
money ultimately determine the new? "It's really, really

tight out there, how can you *not* think about it?"
is her answer, while seated on the sidewalk at the corner

of Wall and Broad across from the illuminated
Stock Exchange, with backpack and smartphone,

mineral water, sleeping bag, bananas, figs,
police vans parked on Nassau, helicopters

circling overhead, her presence digitally monitored.
In a post-bubble credit-collapse environment

three hundred and fifty percent interest rates on payday loans
and the multi-trillion-dollar market in credit default swaps

are history. "Sub-moron"—the assistant district attorney
bursts into laughter—"drops his coin into the pay phone,

then goes and orders retaliation from the Tombs."
Sunday's forecast, the high tide to coincide

with Irene's heavy rains and hurricane-force winds,
sea level to rise four, five feet at the Battery.

ON NATURE

And the puzzles surrounding the cosmological constant,
spacetime imploded into existence. Ten to fifty years
between asbestos breathed and mesothelioma
discovered, a rare form of cancer in the lungs
or heart, or, if in the stomach, spreading
quickly to the liver or spleen. Uploaded
onto one of a half a billion or so blogs: "The human
imagination? A relatively paltry thing, a subproduct,
merely, of the neural activity of a species
of terrestrial primate"; and in another, that other
dimension, the Hudson River, black and still,
the day about to open at the Narrows' edge.
Light on a mountain ash bough, a fresh chill's
blue sensation in the eyes. One week buds, then
the temperature's up and the landscape turns yellow,
in a few days the wind scratches the blossoms,
in a few weeks the sun scorches the leaves.

I, too, see God adumbrations, I, too, write
a book on love. Who, here, appears, to touch the skin.
Hundreds of thousands of square miles of lost
Arctic sea ice, bits of bone on killing grounds,
electromagnetic air. Atrocious and bottomless
states of mind, natural as air.

SYRIA

And when, then, the imagination is transmogrified
into circles of hatred, circles of vengeance
and killing, stealing and deceit? Behind
the global imperia is the interrogation cell. It's not
a good story. Neither the Red Crescent
nor journalists are permitted entry, the women tell
how men and boys are separated, taken in buses
and never seen again, tanks in the streets
with machine guns with no shells in the barrels
because the army fears that those who will use them
might defect. Who knows what has happened,
what is happening, what will happen? God knows.
God knows everything. *The* boy? He is much more
than Mafia; he, and his, own the country. His militias
will fight to the death if for no other reason than
if he's overthrown they will be killed, too. "Iraq,
you remember Iraq, don't you?" she shouts,
a refugee. Her English is good. Reached via Skype,
she speaks anonymously, afraid of repercussions.
"You won't believe what I have seen"—her voice
lowered, almost a whisper—"a decapitated
body with a dog's head sewn on, for example."
Yes, I know, it's much more complicated than that.
"It's the arena right now where the major players are,"
the Chairman of the Joint Chiefs concludes
his exclusive CNN interview. Dagestan—its province

in the North Caucasus—is what the Russians compare
it to, warring clans, sects; Lebanese-like civil war
will break out and spread across the region. Online,
a report—Beirut, the Associated Press—
this morning, "28 minutes ago. 4 Said to Be Dead
at Syrian University," one, Samer Qawass,
thrown, it's said, by pro-regime students
out of the fifth-floor window of his dormitory room,
dying instantly from the fall.

HERE IN A STATE OF TECTONIC TENSION

Its geography similar to Istanbul's—
read for Lake Huron, the Black Sea,
for the St. Clair River, the Bosporus,
for Lake St. Clair, the Sea of Marmara,
for the Detroit River, the Dardanelles,
and for Lake Erie, the Mediterranean—
a natural place for Ford and Olds to open factories,
strategically near the Pittsburgh steel mills, Akron
rubber plants, Mesabi iron ore range.
Here, in ultimate concentration, is industrial
America—Chrysler, Continental, Budd, Hudson,
in an area not much larger than two square miles,
ninety to a hundred thousand employed on two
or three shifts—the capital of a new planet, the one
on wheels. Whacked-out, stamped-out connecting rods,
the steady blown-out flare of furnaces, hammer-die
brought down on anvil-die, oil-holes drilled and oil-
grooves cut—Fordism was Gramsci's word to describe
mass assembly based on systems of specialized
machines operating within organizational domains
of vertically integrated conglomerates fed by small
and medium-sized units coordinated by methods
of marketing exchange—an epical, systemic violence.
Anonymous's eyes pop as he laughs and says
"dragged the old coon from his car, kicked him till
he shit himself, and then we set the auto on fire—God

Jesus was it a show!" How many summers after that
the Motor City burned to the ground? Soon several new
regimes of redistributed wealth would alter the way
capitalism proceeded, a squad of police breaks down
the union hall door, swinging crowbars and tossing canisters
of Mace—around the time the long depression started.
There are stalks of weeds in sunlit snow, an abandoned
house surrounded by acres of snow. The decay apparently
has frightened the smart money away. Metaphorically
underwater—more is owed on properties in Detroit than
they're worth. His hands and feet were bound, found
beaten in a field near Post and Fort, he's in intensive
care at Receiving Hospital, says Sergeant Ollie L. Atkins,
investigators yet to ask him who he is or what happened.
Notice that on the high school baseball diamond is a herd
of goats—attended by whom? Notice, a few doors down,
the stucco-plastered house painted baby blue, walking in front
in a red stocking cap, green specks on his shoes—what
do you think he is thinking? Drive Woodward to Seven Mile,
west on Seven Mile to Hamilton, Hamilton south to the Lodge
Freeway, then the Lodge downtown, and measure the chaos,
drive Mack Avenue east to Seminole, south on Seminole
to Charlevoix, then west on Charlevoix to Van Dyke, south
on Van Dyke to East Jefferson, and remember what isn't.
Ionic pillars carved with grapes and vine leaves no longer
there, deserted houses of gigantic bulk, in which it seems
incredible anyone could ever have lived, no longer there,
Dodge Main's nocturnal gold vapors no longer there,
the constellated bright lights reflected on the Rouge River's

surface no longer there. Narco-capital techno-compressed, gone viral, spread into a state of tectonic tension and freaky abstractions—it'll scare the fuck out of you, is what it'll do, anthropomorphically scaled down by the ferocity of its own obsolescence. Which of an infinity of reasons explain it? Which of an infinity of conflagrations implode its destruction?

AN ANCIENT CLARITY OVERLAID

What is thought and felt, believed and dreamed,
reflected on, the plot worked out in constant

depth, what isn't, for the time being, being written
is being worked on—how long will it be,

the one long poem? Tacitus's *Annals*, its half-
Virgilian lines—Kafka's name on a report,

*Risk Classification and Accident Prevention
in Wartime*—expansion of a tendentious language,

an ancient clarity overlaid. What is said
is, objectively, measured by visual and auditory

standards of the street; as of last Wednesday,
it's said, two hundred six thousand,

six hundred three dead, estimated eighteen million
displaced. How will it end—it won't. Vast open air,

mud-soaked camps, toxic water—no one can say
cluster bombs aren't real. What of my grandparents'

families in Lebanon, in Syria, what of my grandfather,
dead for all but four years of my life, yet

I think of him and talk to him in the present tense.
The beauty of—a scene seen in streetlight.

Rain stopped, she takes my arm, wind icy, gusting,
on Peck Slip, sky streaked velvet. The power of beauty

the proof accorded—so much of her beauty alive in me
to keep me going the time it takes to finish.

Nuance, I know nuance—in her eyes; having
been, will ever be, love in the play of the eyes.

VISIONS OF LABOR

I will have writings written all over it
in human words: wrote Blake. A running
form, Pound's Blake: shouting, whirling
his arms, his eyes rolling, whirling like flaming
cartwheels. Put it this way, in this language:
a blow in the small of the back from a rifle butt,
the crack of a blackjack on a skull, face
beaten to a pulp, punched in the nose
with a fist, glasses flying off, "fuckin' Wobblie
wop, hit him again for me," rifle barrel slammed
against the knees, so much blood in the eyes,
rain, and the night, and the shooting pain
all up and down the spine, can't see. Put it
this way: in the sense of smell is an acrid
odor of scorched metal, in the sense of sound,
the roaring of blowtorches. Put it in this
language: labor's value is abstract value,
abstracted into space in which a milling machine
cutter cuts through the hand, the end of her thumb
nearly sliced off, metal shavings driven in, rapidly
infected. Put it at this point, the point at which
capital is most inhumane, unsentimental,
out of control: the quantity of human labor in
the digital manufacture of a product is progressing
toward the economic value of zero, the maintenance
and monitoring of new cybernetic processes

occupied by fungible, commodified, labor
　　in a form of indentured servitude. Static model,
dynamic model, alternate contract environments,
　　enterprise size and labor market functions,
equilibrium characterization, elasticity of response
　　to productivity shocks: the question in this Third
Industrial Revolution is who owns and controls
　　the data. That's what we're looking at, labor cheap,
replaceable, self-replicating, marginal, contracted out
　　into smaller and smaller units. Them? Hordes
of them, of depleted economic, social value,
　　who don't count, in any situation, in anyone's eyes,
and won't count, ever, no matter what, the truth that,
　　sooner than later, one way or another, they will simply
die off. In Hanover Square, a freezing dawn,
　　inside bronze doors the watchman sips bourbon
and black coffee from a paper cup, sees a drunk or drugged
　　hedge fund boy step over a passed-out body. Logic
of exploitation. Logic of submission; alienation.
　　Eyes fixed on mediated screens, in semiotic
labor flow: how many generations between
　　the age of slavery of these States and ours?
Makers we, of perfectly contemplated machines.

WHO TALKS LIKE THAT?

The Narrows are strips of yellow and jade,
Verrazano Bridge silver, horizontal lines

here; and here, someone alone, afraid, in tears,
sad, sunken eyes, emaciated body; and, here,

the speed of a slap, the strain under the skin;
and this murky and absurdly massive figure

bent double under an unknown burden;
and this bandaged wound, smudged contours,

body and mind breached;
                              and I thought this,

waking early, looking out, the too magnificent
to be described unclouded sky, night still

in the west, the eastern horizon crimson,
melting into blue, light's solid pact being

forged without apotheosis, Governors Island,
series of waves, where the two rivers meet.

Who talks like that? I talk like that. Blinding
point of light in which everything converges

everything is revealed. Dense constellations
of abject suffering, hell-holes, hell-time,

integrated into what's configured. Light
not only looked at, but the light we've

looked with, in common with Byzantine
mosaics, iconic, chromatic, glowing, as if

caught by the sunlit sky, revised, added to, a separate
palette kept for each poem, in the present a presence,

here, a man who watches the woman he loves
walking toward him, in Battery Park, in patches

of light, in the birch leaf green, the harbor
bright blue, in pockets of deep green shade.

IN PARENTHESES

I

As I said, I'm a lawyer. Technically speaking,
is a head blown to pieces by a smart bomb a beheading?

II

Infinitely compressible, yet expandable, time,
and curved space, in the preface to Lucretius's
first book of *De Rerum Natura* is a tribute to Venus,
in the last book a description of the plague.

III

Estimated one to two thousand militia, gangs,
really, of fifteen to three thousand
armed killers, in separate, overlapping
networks, difficult to differentiate, and now this,
to quote an anonymous State Department source,
what no one could have predicted,
this phenomenon's, the caliphate's, rise,
nothing since the triumph
of the Vandals in Roman North Africa
this sudden, this incomprehensible.

IV

In the technocapital sphere
absolute principles of profit growth,
of value accumulation, the absolute freedom
to recombine the production of raw materials
into virtual information
in spaces of time, info-time.

V

A theological-political fragment,
a mythographical, scriptural, text,
and sorrow, to understand the meaning
of sorrow, Saint Sorrow,
the addressee of my avowal,
Saint Sorrow's stern vigil necessary to keep.

VI

Hyperviolence is the word, of epic proportions,
a species thing, the point at which
violence becomes ontology,
these endless ambitious experiments in destruction,
a species grief.

VII

Quite often, almost daily,
in fact, I have strong impressions of eternity,
my ancestors are there, too,
in the shadows—my mother, my father,
grandmothers, grandfathers, whom I refuse
to let perish—whispering to me to be careful.

VIII

What's that about? Someone I heard say
that to say that Hispanics are East Asian
is sort of like saying that Arabs are white.

IX

Hear that, that man's face being stepped on,
skull being cracked by the baton stick, head
slammed against the concrete edge, blood
in his eyes, body limp, in the process now
of being handcuffed.

X

I am speaking of a law, now, understand,
that point at which bodies locked in cages
become ontology, the point at which
structures of cruelty, force, war,
become ontology. The analog
is what I believe in, the reconstruction
of the phenomenology of perception
not according to a machine,
more, now, for the imagination to affix to
than ever before.

IN THIS LANGUAGE, IN WAR'S REVOLUTIONS

In this language, in war's revolutions, voice
in the U-2 spy plane, in the stratosphere;

and, here, pilotless Predators firing Hellfire
missiles, secret surveillance installation, Langley

Air Force Base, millions of hours of high-altitude
photographs, monitored cell phones, classified

instant-messaging; and radar, laser, infrared sensor
information systems, artificial-intelligence-interpreted

drones enabled to carry out analysis in flight,
autonomous weapons, targets selected,

engaged without human intervention, no costly
or difficult to obtain raw materials

required to mass-produce, in a matter of time
bought and sold on the black market. Or,

in the city Baghdad, named Sutis by its founder,
Nebuchadnezzar, here where the prophet Daniel

propounded his dream, a grenade is slipped
in the pocket of each victim, wire linked

to a battery, detonator pressed, bodies blown apart,
the execution party walks away laughing

in clouds of smoke and dust. His family, old money—
a bank, hotels, steel manufacturing, pharmaceuticals—

but listen, he says, this is a country owned
ninety-five percent by a clique, so you do business

with them, then I see him on television,
Nebuchadnezzar, his hair being searched for lice,

patting his cheek as if to identify an aching tooth. Syria,
once the greatest of lands, wrote Pliny;

with its different divisions and names:
the part that borders on Arabia, Palaestina;

and Phoenicia, on the coast of the Phoenician Sea;
and, in its interior, Damascena; and, to the south,

Babylonia; and, between the Tigris and Euphrates,
Mesopotamia; and the parts beyond Mount Taurus,

Sophene and Armenia Adiabene—call it
Syria, geopolitical interests mapped out, reconfigured—

is it proto-world-war now playing out?—
the law of nature playing out is simply

to kill. This killing, in this video, is aestheticized:
pilot, alive, alternated with bodies burned

in strikes, lit powder fuse set to clothes
drenched in gasoline, camera angle close,

terror on the faces gone viral. Look, this is
off the record, Chief of Staff, Air Force,

after his briefing on combined, strategic, international
aerial bombardment, is said to have said,

to truly slow them down you have to take
Ramadi, Mosul, Falluja, Tel Afar, Raqqa.

OF WHAT WE KNOW NOW

And that February cloudless night, deep, now, in its
own reflection, golden full moon's dark blue penumbra;
and ice sheets collapsing causing earthquakes, rattling
seismographs thousands of miles away, mountain-fire
smoke, wind-driven out to sea, enveloping offshore
oil platforms. Violent, narco-state-administered opium
in transit, biomass of manufactured plastics resistant
to decay weighing more than billions of humans—
the violence along social fracture lines, anarcho-capital
circulating at infinite speed, returning to itself even
before taking leave of itself, on its own plane of intelligence,
warping, dissolving nature—the poem in its voracities
of contemplation—the poem's judgment proven, exact—
thought to thought, configurations, in fifty years these words
will be written fifty years ago, that is, now. Spectacles—ugly:
metal molds stuffed with ammonium nitrate, gasoline,
chunks of steel shredded into hot shrapnel on impact,
barrel bombs. Of what we know now, algo-trading in multiple venues,
a third of it run by phantom liquidity providers, turbocharged scalpers;
evidence, irrefutable, in the Commission on Stratigraphy's
Official Report, the Anthropocene (human-driven geological
epoch, never seen before stoichiometric ratios, industrial
metals—cadmium, chromium, nickel, copper, mercury, lead,
zinc—widely and rapidly dispersed into air, earth, water)
beginning around the time I was born; the failure
to apprehend the countless participants in the countless
mass killings, an issue the Mechanism for International
Criminal Tribunals has not, as of yet, effectively addressed.

ON PERIPHERIES OF THE IMPERIUM

I

Eye of the hurricane the Battery, the Hudson
breached, millions of gallons of it
north on West Street filling Brooklyn-Battery
Tunnel, overflowing into the World Trade Center site,
East River, six-to-eight-foot wall of water on South,
Front, Water, John, Fulton, Pearl,
Brooklyn Bridge's woven cables lifted delicately
in hurricane sky.

II

Perhaps I make too much of it, that time,
Eldon Axle, brake plates dipped
in some sort of liquid to protect them from
dust, dirt, metal chips the grinding caused—
that time, night shift, press-machine shop
on Outer Drive, rolls of stainless steel put in,
fixed up, because the work you do is around fire
your cuticles burn if the mask's not on right.

III

When the mind is clear, to hear the sound
of a voice, of voices, shifts in the attitude
of syllables pronounced. When the mind
is clear, to see a Sunday, in August, Shrine
of Our Lady of Consolation, Carey, Ohio,
at a holy water font, a mother washes
her six-year-old's fingers crushed in an accident
so that they'll heal.

IV

So what percentage of Weasel Boy's DNA
do you think is pure weasel? Tooth-twisted,
Yeats's weasels, in "Nineteen Hundred
and Nineteen," fighting in a hole.

V

Conflated, the finance vectors, opaque
cyber-surveillance, supranational cartels,
in the corporate state's political-economic singularity
the greatest number of children
in United States history are, now, incarcerated,
having been sentenced by law.

VI

A comic dimension to it, on this F Train
to One Hundred Sixty-ninth Street
in Queens? He doesn't want to disturb you,
but, see, he was stabbed in the face
with an ice pick, he lost his left eye—
lid pried open with thumb and forefinger—
here, look, he'll show you—
a white-and-pink-colored iris.

IS WHAT IT IS

Fulton near Pearl, dug up to lay the new Fulton Center
subway power lines, a stone wall, three feet high,
in silt-muck seven feet below street level, inside it
a ceramic bird's half-blue, half-yellow head, stem
of a pipe, chunk of glazed seventeenth-century stoneware
decorated with the arms of Amsterdam; huge turkey
vultures taking a liking to the landfill; the preferred source
of food for peregrine falcons is pigeons. His own police
department, the mayor brags, seventh largest army
in the world, and remember, too, the United Nations
is here, so he has his own state department, too, an entrée
into the diplomatic world. Gets deep inside the head, this man
says—he's permanently disabled—affects you emotionally,
what's happened here, pulverized glass, concrete, lead,
asbestos traces, crap, he calls it, here, he shows you
the albuterol and epinephrine he must at all times carry.
To cool your head you walk. Statue of Confucius on
the Bowery, rice-bean cakes, chicken feet, curried squid
on Division, under the Manhattan Bridge, on Canal to Seward
Park, a piece of torn yellow tape tied to a tree, this woman
shouting into her smartphone go fuck yourself and die,
large black letters—in Russian?—on the freighter's hull
fade imperceptibly into one another, the supply route to deliver
food to non-government-held areas in Aleppo severed,
three hundred thousand at risk of starvation—electricity
cut off in markets, houses, schools, bombed hospitals—

migrant smuggling worth more, now, than the trade in drugs
and weapons, profits confined to those in a position
to play, venture capital, private equity, hedge-fund operators,
stock buybacks leveraged, paid for by money borrowed
at artificially low Federal Reserve Bank–charged interest rates,
newly minted Treasury obligations validating private-sector
asset prices into the trillions, statist-sanctioned racketeering—
is what it is. "But after all, I'm a lawyer. So I can never get
away from evil," Kafka said—Franz Kafka, legal officer,
Workers' Accident Insurance Institute, the Kingdom
of Bohemia—whose report *Measures for Preventing
Accidents from Wood-Planing Machines*, among other things,
depicts work-related dissevered fingers. Flint is what it is.
Knowingly to force the poor to purchase and use toxic water
isn't a form of chemical warfare, isn't a form of genocide?

AND FOR THE RECORD

Revelations reoccurring, he who is babbling away
in James Madison Plaza, in what goes around,
what comes around, light made holy by the fury
of the tears with which it mingles, simple enough,
when looked at directly, the child, shy and fearful,
who won't speak. And for the record, the mind,
like the night, has a thousand eyes—
sparrows in the bushes; a small cat
rolls in the snow; sleet pounding the windows.
In the space of a memory, the facade of a church,
an angel on each side of a fiery wheel.

BACK TO THAT

I

Spread on the station's concrete floor,
backpack with files of papers,

water bottles,
a large plastic bag filled with blankets,

spittle dripping from his lips.
Up the stairs to Hillside Avenue,

I look for the Q30 or Q31 bus,
signs in Urdu across the street.

II

And this, now, nuclear
modernization, new

nuclear ordnance and delivery
systems, stealth-missile-firing

submarines, long-range
bombers, steerable

bombs, unprecedented
precision, flexibility,

cost,
one, two

trillion,
to be completed by the hundredth anniversary

of the atomic bombs
unleashed on

Hiroshima,
Nagasaki.

III

The poem of what is touched
incandescently, the poem
measuring out its own circle—lucky poet,
no rules to adhere to,
except never to make an aesthetic mistake.

IV

And in yet another space,
Pasolini's poem

"A un Papa," written
after Pacelli's, Pius XII's, death,

the real evil is not to do good,
wrote Pasolini;

what Pacelli might have done
but did not do—

no greater sinner than Pacelli,
wrote Pasolini.

V

What we felt—
something taken from us
we'll never get back—disarticulated,
no language for it, inwardly unstrung.

VI

Our God, wrote Bonnard,
is light—lucent

greens, bronze-gold
in the river's

silver blaze, pink-black-tinged clouds
dissolving,

darkened purple air.
And to mystery rightly reasoned

a logic consigned,
an intimist's mood,

in our transworld now,
our eyes tell us what

we're doing—
we know exactly

what
we're doing—

in what voice
but a comic voice can the voice

of love
truthfully be?

VII

What's going on—
combination

"Red River Shore,"
"Soon After Midnight,"

song-vibe
is what is going on this

black-gold
October sunset;

you can say what you like
to that.

WHAT MORE IS THERE TO SAY?

December mild, deep January cold,
sunlight filtered through blue haze,

yellow the grass closely pressed,
patches of dirt, in red-and-lavender

twilight, a tugboat in the harbor
clearing the ice. In those circles

in which all heaven breaks loose,
touched by who she is, by what

she wills; in the envisioned heart
inmost issues take the form

of a credo. The God to whom
an account must be rendered,

my dead to whom I pray,
as I, in turn, pray the life once theirs

is transfigured. What a story
to tell, violence from the terror felt,

violence in the suffering, violence
in the mind, collectively modified,

escalated to maximum speed.
So what more is there to say? Many times

the mass of the sun, solar masses
spiraling into spacetime, radiating

energy in gravitational waves, the edges
of the islands soft in the black-gray sky,

on this side of the Battery, near the ferry,
a small bird's footprints, here, in the snow.

New moon, mauve cloud, sea level
higher than normal, the harbor again,

green and gray, punctuated by waves
lashing about. Thickening, the mists,

this early morning; repeated, sounds
of foghorns we hear from afar.

INDEX OF TITLES AND FIRST LINES